VEGETARIAN COOKING OF INDIA

VEGETARIAN
COOKING OF INDIA

TRADITIONS • INGREDIENTS • TASTES • TECHNIQUES • 80 CLASSIC RECIPES

Mridula Baljekar
Photography by Jon Whitaker

southwater

This edition is published by Southwater, an imprint of Anness Publishing Ltd, 108 Great Russell Street, London WC1B 3NA; info@anness.com

www.southwaterbooks.com; www.annesspublishing.com;
twitter: @Anness_Books

If you like the images in this book and would like to investigate using them for publishing, promotions or advertising, please visit our website www.practicalpictures.com for more information.

© Anness Publishing Ltd 2015

Publisher: Joanna Lorenz
Editorial Director: Helen Sudell
Project Editor: Melanie Hibbert
Designer: Lisa Tai
Photography: Jon Whitaker
Food Stylist: Joy Skipper
Prop Stylist: Penny Markham
Production Controller: Pirong Wang

PUBLISHER'S NOTE
Although the advice and information in this book are believed to be accurate and true at the time of going to press, neither the authors nor the publisher can accept any legal responsibility or liability for any errors or omissions that may have been made nor for any inaccuracies nor for any loss, harm or injury that comes about from following instructions or advice in this book.

NOTES
- Bracketed terms are intended for American readers.
- For all recipes, quantities are given in both metric and imperial measures and, where appropriate, in standard cups and spoons. Follow one set of measures, but not a mixture, because they are not interchangeable.
- Standard spoon and cup measures are level.
  1 tsp = 5ml, 1 tbsp = 15ml, 1 cup = 250ml/8fl oz.
- Australian standard tablespoons are 20ml. Australian readers should use 3 tsp in place of 1 tbsp for measuring small quantities.
- American pints are 16fl oz/2 cups. American readers should use 20fl oz/ 2.5 cups in place of 1 pint when measuring liquids.
- Electric oven temperatures in this book are for conventional ovens. When using a fan oven, the temperature will probably need to be reduced by about 10-20°C/20-40°F. Since ovens vary, you should check with your manufacturer's instruction book for guidance.
- The nutritional analysis given for each recipe is calculated per portion (i.e. serving or item), unless otherwise stated. If the recipe gives a range, such as Serves 4-6, then the nutritional analysis will be for the smaller portion size, i.e. 6 servings. The analysis does not include optional ingredients, such as salt added to taste.
- Medium (US large) eggs are used unless otherwise stated.

Front cover shows Stuffed Sweet Peppers – for recipe, see page 29.

PICTURE ACKNOWLEDGEMENTS:
The publisher would like to thank Jon Whitaker for his stunning photography throughout the book, apart from the following images: Alamy pages 6, 7t, 8, 9t, 9bl, 9br, 11, 12br, 13, 20bl, 20br; and Matt Munro for author portrait on the jacket.

CONTENTS

Introduction

Indian dishes are adored throughout the world and vegetarianism has long been a main feature of this popular cuisine. Vegetarian Indian food offers so many combinations of tastes and aromas that it never becomes bland or predictable. Vibrant vegetables in rich fragrant sauces; nutty lentils, beans and peas; and of course an incredible array of spices: these characterize exciting recipes that warm the body and soothe the soul. Besides offering fabulous flavours, the dishes are also extremely fresh and healthy.

The vast and vibrant land of India conjures up images of mystery, magic and romance. It is a land steeped in heritage and history, one that has witnessed great empires rise and crumble.

Exotic spices have been grown in India for centuries, and it is the carefully prepared blends of these spices that provide the mouthwatering tastes and aromas of countless vegetarian dishes eaten throughout the entire country.

India has long been known as the spice bowl of the world. The use of premium quality aromatics in this sun-drenched, monsoon-fed land was an established way of life long before the traders arrived. Among those lured to the country by valuable spices were Arabs, English, Dutch, Portuguese and Spanish traders.

Religious influences

There are many religions in India that advocate non-violence and believe eating the flesh of an animal to be detrimental to the person's spiritual welfare. Following a vegetarian diet on the other hand is thought to promote good health and clear thinking power.

Hinduism is the major religion of the country and around 30 per cent of Hindus are vegetarian. Strict Hindus would not take the life of an animal in order to satisfy their own needs as this would go against all beliefs. The members of the highest caste within the Hindu community, known as the Brahmins, are the most stringent followers of vegetarianism. They do not eat eggs, and avoid strong-smelling ingredients, such as onion and garlic, as these are generally associated with cooking meat, poultry and fish. However, some Hindus do include fish and shellfish in their diet, believing these to be the fruits of the sea and thus equivalent to the vegetables grown on land.

A rich and varied cuisine

Foreign travellers introduced cooking techniques that are still practised today. The north continues to be dominated by Mughal cuisine, while the east has tribal and Anglo-Indian influences. In the south, Syrian Jews and French traders passed on their cooking techniques, and western India came under the influence of the Portuguese and the Persians (Parsis). The result is a rich, colourful and multi-dimensional cuisine with a repertoire of recipes that is virtually unmatched anywhere else in the world.

Spectacular scenery, fascinating ancient customs and glorious foods all continue to draw foreigners to this magical land. Just like the breathtakingly beautiful scenery, culinary traditions have been influenced by

LEFT Barbecued corn on the cob is a popular snack sold by street vendors.

geographical and climatic conditions. With vast distances to be travelled, and no means of transporting fresh produce efficiently, cooks have made the best use of the ingredients available to them locally.

The beauty of Indian cooking is in its variety. Different areas and traditions have developed their own regional specialities, and recipes have been handed down through the generations. Although many dishes are fiery with chillies, there are others that are mellow. Many of the most familiar regional dishes we enjoy come from northern India. These include koftas, mild kormas and tandoori recipes. The cuisine of north-west Province, which is now in Pakistan, is beautifully aromatic, but does not use chillies excessively, so it is not too hot.

The most fiery spice blends, such as the famous vindaloo, originate from western India. The recipes of west India tend to favour the use of dairy products including yogurt and buttermilk, and the meals are typically accompanied by all kinds of unusual pickles. Coconuts are favourite ingredients of eastern and southern India,

and are used for making both sweet and savoury dishes, including deliciously creamy sauces. As south Indian cuisine is predominantly vegetarian, there is no shortage of delectable meat-free recipes to choose from, which utilize nuts, beans, peas and lentils, making hearty and nutritious meals to appeal to both vegetarians and meat-eaters alike.

Vegetarianism for health

Indian vegetarian cooking aims to produce a balanced, healthy and appetizing meal. A vegetarian diet consists of good quality protein and high-fibre foods with all the essential vitamins and nutrients. The main sources of protein for vegetarians are beans, peas, lentils, grains and dairy products. Indian cooks use these in numerous ways to make delicious and varied meals. Fresh vegetables provide all the vitamins and minerals that the body needs every day. Even the daily bread, chapati, is made of wholemeal (whole-

LEFT Beans, peas and lentils are essential protein sources for vegetarians.

ABOVE A stunning mountainside tea estate in Kerala, south India.

wheat) flour, which has a high percentage of bran and wheatgerm, and this provides the necessary intake of fibre and protein.

Vegetarian meals are on the whole inexpensive and quick to cook. A vast number of India's population live on a daily diet of lentils, beans, pulses, fresh vegetables, chapatis and rice. The numerous different ways in which they can be cooked stops the diet from becoming too monotonous.

Following a vegetarian diet does not have to mean limiting the body's intake of essential nutrients because combining protein with vitamins and minerals is really easy. Lentils, peas, beans and dairy items provide plenty of protein, and fresh fruit and vegetables are a great source of vitamins and minerals. Rice is a good source of carbohydrate, which is also believed to steady blood sugar levels. The cooking process mainly uses light oils such as sunflower or vegetable oils, which are important in maintaining good health.

Fat is a wonderful flavour enhancer as well as a great source of energy. We all need small amounts of it for the repair and growth of cells, although excessive amounts have well-known negative effects on our bodies.

Many of the popular ingredients used in Indian vegetarian cooking claim to have medicinal powers. For example, garlic has antiseptic properties that aid the digestive system and is excellent for lowering the blood cholesterol levels and reducing the risk of heart disease. Fresh ginger reduces stomach acidity and combat the risk of ulcers, while cinnamon, cardamom and cloves are good for fighting the symptoms of coughs and colds.

Planning an Indian vegetarian meal

Rice and bread are the staples of an Indian vegetarian diet while the main vegetable dish is often served with a platter of inviting little side dishes, such as pickles, chutneys and salads flavoured with fresh herbs, chillies or yogurt.

Traditionally, Indian dishes are not strictly categorized into starters and main courses. Several dishes are cooked and served at the same time and the diners simply help themselves to everything. What is more, people generally have second helpings of everything on offer! It is, however, customary to start the meal with bread and follow with rice, both of these

accompanied by spicy dishes. In the classic style, all the food is served on a *thali* (large platter) traditionally made of stainless steel. Rice and bread are placed on the *thali*, with small bowls containing various curries. Pickles, chutneys and raitas are also served on the platter.

A meal will usually end with fresh fruit, rather than elaborate or cooked desserts. Fruits can be served with real flair, however, and are often combined with other ingredients to create imaginative and exciting flavours. Choose one or two exotic

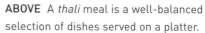

ABOVE A *thali* meal is a well-balanced selection of dishes served on a platter.

fruits, such as papaya, pomegranate or star fruit, and combine them with everyday fruits for a zingy salad. Serve with Greek (US strained plain) yogurt flavoured with rose water and a little ground cardamom.

Indian sweets (candies) tend to be quite rich so are more commonly served as a snack with tea and coffee.

Until recent years alcoholic drinks did not accompany an Indian meal. This is because most Indians prefer to drink only refreshing water or a cooling yogurt drink (lassi) with their meal. This is a practice that is now changing since beer, lager and wine are becoming more popular and readily available accompaniments to food. India now produces very good quality wines, which complement spicy food, and there are also plenty of light white wines or low-tannin reds from other countries that go equally well with Indian food. Fiery dishes are best accompanied by a really well-chilled and full-bodied white wine. Tea and coffee are traditionally enjoyed after a meal, and hot or chilled spiced tea is a particular favourite throughout India.

LEFT A colourful selection of spices on sale in an open-air market in Goa, India.

LEFT A classic dish of vegetable dhansak presented in a large pewter serving bowl.

desserts. It also includes a variety of side dishes, salads, chutneys and relishes, as well as breads, rices and drinks – in fact, everything you need to create the perfect meal, whether it be a light supper or a more elaborate dinner party for friends and family.

Many recipes are quick to prepare with the simplest of spice combinations, whereas others call for a more varied store of spices and flavourings, including some lesser-known ingredients such as mango powder (amchur) and compressed tamarind. Today most of these special ingredients are readily available from supermarkets. Fresh herbs such as coriander (cilantro) are sold cheaply in large bunches in Asian stores and markets. These stores also sell large bags of whole spices which will provide you with a plentiful supply for flavouring all your favourite Indian dishes and are ideal if you enjoy preparing spicy food regularly.

Many of the culinary skills and expertise widely used around the world today were originally developed in India, and a selection of the best regional cuisine is featured in this wonderful collection of vegetarian Indian recipes.

If planning a party, it is a good idea to cook the main dishes a day ahead of the event, storing them in the refrigerator until you are ready to reheat them. Accompanying dishes can also be prepared 24 hours in advance, although the seasonings should not be added until just before serving. You can prepare vegetables in advance but do not cook them more than a few hours ahead. Likewise, you can prepare ingredients for raitas a day ahead, but do not assemble them until a few hours before they are needed; the yogurt for raitas should always be fresh.

How to use this book

This recipe book is divided into regional sections that represent the best of the different vegetarian cuisines of India, from snacks and starters to main dishes and

BELOW A beautiful violet aubergine growing in Akola, Maharashtra.

BELOW Coconut is a favourite south-Indian ingredient, particularly in Kerala.

BELOW Red-hot chilli growing in the spice fields of Andhra Pradesh, south India.

A land of contrasts

India is an immense country with an extremely varied landscape and climate, from the mighty snow-clad Himalayas in the extreme north, through the wonderfully fertile flatlands of the Indus and Ganges rivers and the sandy wastes of the deserts of Rajasthan, to the tropical forests of the south. India boasts bustling modern cities that embrace the 21st century alongside rural farming communities where the age-old traditions of cooking and agriculture are preserved.

The rugged north

North India contains the highest mountain range in the world, the Himalayas (meaning 'abode of snow'). In Kashmir, the contrasts created by the magnificent mountain ranges and the lush green valleys dotted with lakes are a visual delight. The state is well known for its sweet, juicy fruit and nuts, which thrive in the cool mountain climate. During the summer months, Kashmiri lakes are also host to floating fruit and vegetable gardens where tomatoes, watermelons, cucumbers and herbs are grown.

Himachal Pradesh is popularly known as 'the mountain state' – with plenty of locally grown fruits, vegetables and spices, and the clean mountain air, the locals have a remarkably healthy environment. Further south, the basmati rice grown in the Dehra Dun area of Uttar Pradesh is one of the most prized crops in the whole country.

The small state of Punjab, with its five major rivers ('punj' meaning five and 'ab' meaning river or water) is situated at the foothills of the Himalayas. Winter food here is warm and spicy, and in the scorching summer many Punjabis start their day with a glass of lassi, a cooling yogurt drink.

The capital city, Delhi, which lies in the north of India, was founded in the 11th century. Old Delhi's vast imperial buildings, such as the famous Red Fort, lie alongside a network of crowded markets and narrow alleys. The city is dotted with roadside stalls that sell irresistible kebabs, naan and vegetarian snacks with deliciously spiced chutneys. Delhi is truly the gourmet city of India, with a rich and varied cuisine.

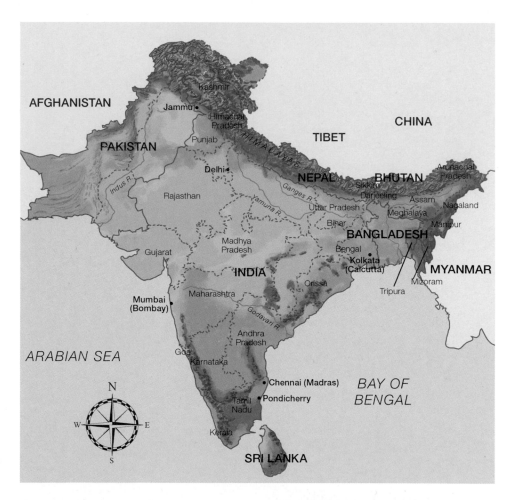

The seven sisters

The north-eastern part of India is a large area made up of seven small states, including Assam and Sikkim, called the 'seven sisters'. Each of these states is strikingly individual and beautiful, with its own cultures and traditions. Bordering with Bhutan, China, Bangladesh and Myanmar (Burma), the north-east is India's true frontier region.

Assam nestles in the foothills of the Himalayas and has a temperate climate

ABOVE India is a vast country boasting diverse landscapes and climates.

that is ideal for cultivating its world-famous tea crops. Assamese cuisine is simple and healthy, with very little fat being used in the cooking process. The emphasis is on dishes containing plenty of fresh vegetables. Greens and pulses flavoured with garlic, mustard oil and chillies feature regularly.

The majestic east

East India stretches from the Ganges plains to the magnificent eastern Himalayas. The typical combination of five spices known as panchforon, with its intensely aromatic flavour, is at the heart of Bengal's simple, delicious vegetable dishes. Perhaps Bengal's greatest contribution to the food heritage of India is its magnificent spectrum of sweets, which include a delicate rice pudding flavoured with cardamom and cinnamon.

The warm south

South India looks serene and beautiful, with swaying coconut palm trees, golden beaches and lush tropical scenery. The South Indian economy thrives on spices, rice, tea, coffee and coconut. The state of Andhra Pradesh is particularly noted for its chilli crops, which include the famed Guntur red chillies, known for their pungency. The food of this region is quite fiery, but cooling dishes with a neutralizing effect are always served in combination with hot spicy food.

Kerala is one of India's smallest states, representing only 1.8 per cent of the total area of India, and is a land of exuberant beauty. Fish and shellfish dishes are naturally popular in this watery state, along with a vast range of vegetables cooked in spicy coconut milk and served with rice.

The agricultural centre

Madhya Pradesh, often described as India's undiscovered heartland, is also one of the country's largest states. Beautiful hill ranges overlook the Ganges plain, and the black volcanic soil is very fertile. There is no definitive cuisine style of this area, but it borrows heavily from neighbouring states such as Gujarat, Rajasthan and Bihar. The economy of Madhya Pradesh relies heavily upon agriculture, and especially important crops include rice, wheat, sorghum and coarse millet. Although rice is popular, wheat is the staple food in the drier western areas where it grows more abundantly.

RIGHT Houseboats moored on a palm-fringed lake in Kerala, south India.

The vibrant west

Western India contains a breathtaking variety of landscapes, with tidal mudflats, steep ravines and beautiful beaches. The north-western state of Rajasthan, an arid land near the border with Pakistan, is the home of maharajahs (emperors) and rajputs (princes), and has a long tradition of distinctive and elaborate royal cuisine.

To the south of Rajasthan, the people in Gujarat have developed and mastered the

ABOVE An Assamese tea picker gathers leaves in a basket strapped to her head.

true art of vegetarian cooking, and rely on yogurt and buttermilk as a source of protein.

Further south lies the tiny state of Goa, which has a food culture that is a perfect marriage of Eastern ingredients with Western cooking styles, arising from the influence of the Portuguese traders who first arrived here in the late 15th century.

Indian festivals and celebrations

India is a spiritual land comprised of many religions: Hindu, Muslim, Christian, Sikh, Jain and Buddhist. It is, therefore, not too surprising that Indian culture is rich with numerous vibrant and joyful festivals and celebrations. However, the vast majority of the religious holidays celebrated in the 21st century are Hindu in origin. Most of these events have elaborate stories and rituals associated with them, not to mention fantastic food to accompany each celebration.

Religious food culture

The influence of religion on Indian food has been profound. The two main religions, Hinduism and Islam, have certain taboos: for example, Hindus do not eat beef as the cow was the sacred companion of Lord Krishna, and Muslims are prohibited from eating pork or drinking alcohol according to their holy book, the Koran. Sikhs, Jains and Buddhists have certain food rules in common with Hindus, but also have distinctive food cultures of their own.

There is a stunning variety of festival foods in India to accompany the many major festivals held every year. In the Hindu religion, more than one god and goddess is worshipped, and each one is believed to be the patron of a particular profession or trade. A farmer may offer the gods of sun and rain their favourite dishes, for example, so that they will bless him with a fruitful harvest.

Rice, ghee (clarified butter), sugar, milk, yogurt and honey are considered to be the purest foods. They are also thought to have spiritual qualities, hence the practice of cooking sweet dishes and offering them at the altar before distributing them to family and friends. Throughout the country rice pudding is given as a holy offering, and nuts, cardamom and saffron are added to this delicious creamy dessert.

Harvest festivals

At the beginning of the year, the two Hindu harvest festivals, known as Lohri and Baisakhi, are celebrated in northern India. Lohri is celebrated by the people of the Punjab in January and Baisakhi follows in April. It is customary to serve dried fruits, sweetmeats and spicy savoury snacks similar to Bombay mix, as well as a spicy dish of mustard greens (sarson ka saag) and flat breads made of cornmeal (makki ki roti).

The people of Tamil Nadu in south India celebrate their harvest festival, *Pongal*, for four days each year, starting on 13 January. *Pongal* in the Tamil language means 'boiling over', which signifies prosperity due to a bountiful crop. The food cooked during *Pongal* is totally vegetarian. The special dish of the day is known as khichri, which is a combination of rice, milk and jaggery (unrefined palm sugar). It is cooked in a pot called a *Pongal panai*.

January sees another harvest festival in the north-eastern state of Assam. This is known as Bihu, when a good harvest is celebrated with family and friends by lighting an early morning bonfire and cooking yams in the burning ashes.

Spring festivals

Holi, the festival of colours, brings a special feast for the entire family and friends. Sweetmeats, savoury snacks such as vadai (lentil fritters) and papri (a crisp bread made of chickpea flour) are made. It is also a tradition for parents to present new clothes in bright colours to a daughter and her children.

Autumn festivals

Durga Puja is a major Hindu festival celebrated all over India in the autumn. The goddess Durga is believed to be the defeater of evil, and the festival

ABOVE Creamy Indian rice pudding scented with saffron, cardamom and nutmeg.

ABOVE Khichri boiling in a *Pongal panai* at a village harvest festival in Tamil Nadu.

ABOVE A mixed selection of sweets ready to share at a Diwali celebration.

ABOVE A colourful plateful of soft fudge-like sweetmeats known as burfi.

ABOVE Female folk dancers celebrate a *Pongal* festival in a village in Tamil Nadu.

commemorates her triumph over the wicked demon Mahisasur. Food such as deep-fried puffed bread, spiced potatoes, fragrant lentils and different kinds of sweets are offered at the altar and then shared between everyone present.

Onam is a festival mainly celebrated in Kerala, South India. It marks the end of the monsoon season, but legends and myths have a strong influence in India and Onam also celebrates the life of King Mahabali, a past ruler of Kerala. The Onam feast is traditionally served on banana leaves, and consists of fish and seafood cooked in spicy coconut broth, chutneys made with coconut and spices, plenty of spicy vegetables and rice.

Diwali, the biggest Hindu festival, is also celebrated over five days in the autumn. It commemorates the return of the Hindu prince Rama from 14 years of exile. Rama was supposed to have returned in the evening and oil lamps are lit everywhere to welcome him, hence the name Diwali, meaning 'festival of lights'. During Diwali sweets are the most important foods. In keeping with the Hindu belief that exchanging sweets among

family and friends represents inner goodness, many varieties of sweets made of coconut are made and distributed.

Raksha Bandhan is another major festival in India that is mainly celebrated in the north and west. On this day, a sacred thread is tied to a brother's wrist by his sister to signify her love for him, and she offers special prayers for her brother's welfare. The brother in turn pledges to love and protect his sister in any circumstances,

strengthening the bond between them. The brother gives gifts to his sister and she cooks an elaborate meal which the entire family shares. Such delights as fruit and vegetable patties, soft fudge (burfi), sweet dumplings (malpua) and cardamom-scented vermicelli pudding are part of the feast.

Whatever the festival, sweets always feature prominently, as Indians believe that they spread love and goodwill.

RIGHT Coloured rice powder is used during festivals to create patterns on the streets.

Classic ingredients

Spices are an integral part of all Indian cuisine and really bring the food to life. The art of blending spices in subtle combinations is one that Indian cooks have mastered over the centuries. Regional variations make their story a fascinating one, with locally grown herbs and spices at the heart of many a delicious dish. Certain ingredients, such as onion, ginger and garlic, are also found in almost every Indian recipe and are the absolute basics of all aromatic and flavoursome meals.

Spices and condiments

The range of Indian spices and condiments is extensive and varied, and the art of selecting and using the spices for a specific dish has evolved through the generations. The chosen spices should complement the dish and enhance the taste and flavour of the main ingredients without masking them. For instance, a vegetable curry should have an aromatic, rounded flavour, but the natural taste of the vegetables should still predominate over the spices.

In general, ground spices such as cinnamon, cumin and turmeric add colour and taste, and integrate totally into the sauce. Whole spices such as cinnamon sticks, whole cardamom seeds and whole chillies, on the other hand, add flavour and perfume to a dish but do not blend into the sauce.

Ajowan This is an important ingredient in vegetarian cooking. It is used with most root vegetables, and in north India a few ajowan seeds are added to the dough when making flat breads such as chapatis. It also complements food that can be hard to digest, such as beans, peas and lentils.

Aniseed These liquorice-flavoured sweet seeds are used in the preparation of many fried and deep-fried Indian dishes as an aid to digestion.

Asafoetida This powerful, aromatic spice is used extensively in cooking the pulses that are so essential in a vegetarian diet. Used in minute quantities for its anti-flatulent properties, it is added to hot oil, which mellows its overpowering smell and complements the dish.

Cardamom, cinnamon and cloves These three spices are an indispensable part of Indian cooking. Southern India produces an abundance of cardamom, and south Indians use it deftly in its ground form in their desserts and sweetmeats, while north Indians are passionate about its sweet, heady aroma in chicken dishes, pilaus and biryanis. Cardamom, cinnamon and cloves are also the primary ingredients in garam masala.

Chillies It is surprising that chillies were not known in India until the 16th century, when the Portuguese introduced them to south India. They soon became a favourite ingredient and today Indian cuisine is synonymous with chillies. South Indians are probably the biggest consumers of chillies; their food is renowned for its pungency,

ABOVE Asafoetida can be overpowering so it should always be used sparingly.

ABOVE Cardamom seeds can be used whole or crushed to add aroma to dishes.

ABOVE It is worth keeping a supply of dried chillies to add an instant kick to recipes.

ABOVE Garlic is a store-cupboard essential as it is a basic flavour enhancer.

ABOVE The nutty taste of mustard seeds enhances the flavour of many lentil dishes.

ABOVE Saffron is pricey but well worth the investment as you only need a few strands.

and dried red chillies are a vital ingredient here. They are used in a hot oil seasoning to add a superb flavour to vegetables, lentils and chutneys. Chilli powder is used widely all over India.

Coriander and cumin seeds These are part of every savoury dish in India. Coriander, with its sweet, mellow flavour, is used in many vegetable curries, and cumin is its traditional companion. In north India zeera aloo (cumin potatoes) is a great favourite, with the predominating flavour of cumin. Korma dishes, on the other hand, generally have generous quantities of coriander with little or no cumin.

Fennel seeds These are used in many vegetarian dishes to add a warm, sweet flavour. They are also good for alleviating stomach ailments. Fennel is one of the ingredients used in eastern and north-eastern India to make five-spice mix (panchforon).

Fenugreek These tiny pale cream seeds have a powerful aroma with a lingering bitter taste, but when dropped in hot oil, they mellow and add a distinctive taste to the dish. In the Karnataka district of southern India, a combination of roasted fenugreek

and dried red chillies is used in a dish known as ambat, which gives an incredibly aromatic flavour to the lentils and vegetables used. Fresh fenugreek leaves are used as a vegetable, while the dried leaves are used in delicious sauces and breads, and also combine well with potatoes and spinach.

Garam masala There is no set recipe for this mixture of spices, but a typical mixture might include peppercorns, black cumin seeds, cloves, cinnamon and black cardamom pods.

Mustard seeds These delicious seeds are a key ingredient used in cooking Indian vegetable and lentil dishes. They are used right at the beginning of the cooking process, and are added to very hot oil to release their nutty flavour into it. There are three varieties of mustard seeds: pale, medium brown and black, all of them grown in India. In the south, a mixture of mustard seeds, cumin seeds, curry leaves and dried red chillies is commonly used in vegetarian cooking, whereas in Bengal and Assam, mustard seeds are combined with cumin, fennel and nigella seeds to flavour many vegetable and lentil dishes, a combination which produces an unforgettable aromatic taste.

Nigella This aromatic spice has a sharp and tingling taste and is used mainly to add flavour to vegetables and pulses.

Nutmeg and mace The nutmeg plant is unique in that it produces two spices in one: nutmeg and mace (javitri). These are both highly aromatic spices and are used extensively in northern cuisine.

Onion, ginger and garlic These are the most common ingredients in any Indian dish, but the methods of preparation and cooking vary. Onion, ginger and garlic are used as an all-in-one paste in certain dishes, while for others, onions are boiled and puréed before being cooked with ginger, garlic and dry spices. Browned onion purée is another way of creating a distinctive flavour.

Saffron The stigmas of the saffron crocus flower are hand-picked and sun-dried before being packaged for commercial use. They are so light that it takes about 500,000 dried stigmas to make 450g/1lb of saffron. A few strands soaked in a little milk or water will give any dish an exotic appearance and taste. Saffron brings a magic touch to north Indian vegetable kormas, pilaus, biryanis, rice, vermicelli desserts and certain breads.

ABOVE Vibrant turmeric is quite a powerful spice so only a tiny amount is needed.

ABOVE Fresh coriander leaves add colour and a distinctive flavour to many recipes.

ABOVE Caramelized basmati rice is a traditional accompaniment to a dhansak.

Star anise This is a star-shaped liquorice-flavoured pod. The spice is commonly used in the preparation of biryani dishes in the southern Indian state of Andhra Pradesh.

Turmeric The golden hue of turmeric, which brings all Indian dishes to life, lends a rich colour to vegetables and pulses and adds an earthy flavour. On its own it has a bitter taste, which disappears when blended with other ingredients. Turmeric is highly antiseptic, with exceptional preserving qualities.

Herbs

Many Indian cooks will not consider serving a dish without a handful of fresh coriander (cilantro). The leaves of this fragrant plant are used to garnish almost every savoury dish. Curry leaves also play an important part in south Indian cooking.

Other flavourings

Sweet, sour, salty, pungent and bitter tastes are all important in Indian cooking. Jaggery (unrefined palm sugar) is traditionally used for a sweet taste. There are several souring agents, but the most commonly used ones are tamarind and dried mango powder. They each impart their own distinctive

taste and flavour to a dish. The versatile mango is indigenous to India. It is used in curries at different stages of ripeness, but the unripe fruit is also sun-dried and ground into a dry powder called amchur. This sour-tasting powder is sprinkled over dishes as a garnish; it is not used in cooking.

Staple foods

Rice and bread are the two staple foods in India. Rice grows in areas of abundant rainfall in the south, west and east, and it is a vital part of the daily diet of the people in these areas. Wheat needs a drier, colder climate and northern India is ideal for this. Rice provides the daily amount of required starch while bread has plenty of dietary fibre.

Rice This crop has been grown in India since at least 1900BC. Among the different types of long grain rice used, basmati is the most popular. Due to its natural aroma and unique taste, it is considered to be the king of all long grain rice. The name basmati means 'full of fragrance'.

Basmati rice varies a great deal in quality, and like a good wine, it often depends on how long the rice has been allowed to mature. Unlike other long grain

rice, basmati is stored under carefully controlled conditions for several years before being distributed for commercial use. The longer the rice is matured, the better its taste, texture and flavour. Mature rice will cook without sticking, producing beautifully dry and fluffy grains, while young rice usually has a higher proportion of starch, which makes it prone to sticking. Generally, the best basmati rice comes from the snow-fed paddy fields at the foot of the Himalayas.

Indian cuisine uses rice in many ways, from the very plain to the utterly exotic. Fabulous biryanis and simple flavoured rice dishes are all cooked to perfection, transforming the grains into a delight for a gourmet's palate. It is also ground into rice flour (used in making sweets, dumplings and pancakes), flattened into flaked rice or puffed at a high temperature to make delicious snacks and sweets.

Rice also has religious and social significance in India. It is considered a holy food, and Indians will often make a *prasad* (sacred offering) of cooked rice, milk and sugar. In Hindu mythology, rice is depicted as a symbol of good fortune and fertility. On the arrival of a Hindu bridegroom at his bride's house for the wedding ceremony,

ABOVE Chapatis are the everyday breads eaten within most Indian households.

ABOVE Ghee is a cooking fat traditionally used in Indian kitchens.

small handfuls of rice, rather like confetti, are thrown over him to welcome him. At the end of the ceremony, when the bride leaves her parents' home and arrives at her husband's, she is offered a large bowl of rice. Before entering her new husband's house, she scatters some of it on the ground to indicate that she brings good fortune with her.

Bread This is an important daily food, especially in northern India, where the climate is cooler and ideal for wheat production. North Indians thrive on a daily diet of numerous kinds of bread with their curries. They are generally made from the same three ingredients: grains, salt and water. Unleavened flat breads, ranging from simple, fat-free chapatis to rich, layered parathas (similar to flaky pastry), are made from wheat. Chapatis are dry-roasted, but there are other flat breads to which a small amount of oil or ghee is added during cooking. Leavened breads such as naan, of which there are numerous varieties, are generally commercially made nowadays.

In India, especially in the rural parts, people grind their own wheat to make flour, and bake their bread on a cast-iron griddle. The wheat flour, known as atta, is very fine and is made by grinding the entire wheat kernel, which is packed with all essential nutrients, including a high proportion of roughage. As well as wheat flour, breads are also made from rice flour, maize flour, gram flour, ground barley, and even semolina.

Cooking fats In days gone by, most cooks in India used ghee (clarified butter) to cook with, but now that people are more aware of the damaging effects of saturated fats, many have switched to using oil. Any light cooking oil such as sunflower oil or plain olive oil is ideal for use in Indian dishes.

Paneer Indian cheese is a highly nourishing, protein-rich ingredient around which a dazzling array of vegetarian dishes have been created. North India's signature dish, matter paneer, is a delicious combination of paneer and garden peas in a richly spiced tomato sauce. Another well-known and much-loved North Indian paneer dish is methi chaman (paneer with spinach and fenugreek leaves). Paneer is traditionally a home-made cheese, full of all the goodness of protein and calcium, and providing as much protein as meat, poultry and fish.

Cucumber Raita

This slightly sour, yogurt-based accompaniment has a refreshing, cooling effect on the palate when eaten with spicy foods. A cucumber raita will also help to balance the flavours of an Indian meal.

Makes about 600ml/1 pint/2½ cups

½ cucumber

1 fresh green chilli, seeded and chopped

300ml/½ pint/1¼ cups natural (plain) yogurt

1.5ml/¼ tsp salt

1.5ml/¼ tsp ground cumin

1 Dice the cucumber finely and place in a large mixing bowl. Add the chilli.

2 Gently beat the natural yogurt with a fork until it becomes smooth. Then stir it into the cucumber and chilli mixture.

3 Next, stir in the salt and cumin. Cover the bowl with clear film (plastic wrap) and leave in the refrigerator to chill before serving.

Cooking tools and techniques

Throughout India, different types of equipment, together with varied techniques of cooking, are used to produce the flavours, colours and textures that are characteristic to each regional dish. Using the appropriate pans to cook vegetarian dishes helps to create a delicate balance of flavours. Many Indian cooks have a range of heavy pans and shaped utensils at their disposal, but with a little care in selecting the right shape and weight, alternatives that work just as well can always be found in the modern kitchen.

Cooking utensils

There is a vast array of favourite cooking utensils in India. All along the southern coastal regions, terracotta cooking pots are preferred. These tend to be unglazed as aeration is easier; this means that the food does not need immediate refrigeration in spite of the extreme heat in the south. In the north, the emphasis is more on sealing cooking pots well so that the flavour of the food is concentrated inside – a method of cooking known as *dum*. Most traditional Indian cooking is done in heavy cast-iron, steel or copper cooking pots and pans. These help to distribute the heat evenly, cooking the food without losing any of the natural moisture and allowing the spices to be pre-fried without sticking to the bottom of the pan.

Handi A *handi* is used to cook many steamed dishes. It is a copper pot with a neck that is narrower than the base, a somewhat bigger version of a *degchi*. Decorated ovenproof *handis* are now available and they have become a favourite in the modern Indian kitchen.

Kadhai/karahi Fried puffed breads (puri and luchi) are deep-fried in a round-bottomed pan, similar to a wok, known as a *kadhai* or *karahi*. A *kadhai* is also needed to produce all types of bhuna (stir-fried) dishes – an amazing range of mouth-watering dishes have been created, based on this humble cooking utensil. The *kadhai* is probably one of the oldest kinds of cooking pans in India – archeologists have discovered the ancient remains of a pan

that closely resembles the *kadhai*. Today this pan is a common sight in every domestic and restaurant kitchen and every street-side eatery in north India and Pakistan.

Patila A heavy steel pan with a lid, known as a *patila*, is used for making stock, kormas and bhuna dishes. Kormas need heavy cooking pots with tight-fitting lids, as very little liquid is used during the cooking process. *Korma*, which means braising, is essentially a technique of cooking rather than a particular dish.

Lagan A shallow copper utensil known as a *lagan* is used for cooking certain *dum* dishes in Lucknow, northern India. The lagan has a slightly rounded bottom and a heavy, tight-fitting lid. The temperature

ABOVE *Handi* pots, often made of copper, are narrower at the neck than at the base.

ABOVE The wok-like *kadhai* is used to make stir-fried curries and fried puff bread.

ABOVE A *patila* is a heavy pan with a lid, often used for making stocks and kormas.

must be kept quite gentle, and indirect heat is created by placing burning charcoal on the lid. This method can easily be replicated using a casserole dish in a low oven, as long as the dish is sealed well.

Degchi Pilaus and biryanis require a special shape of cooking pot, as the food is cooked entirely in steam, producing fabulous flavours. This pot, known as a *degchi*, is pear-shaped and can be made of either brass or copper. The narrow neck helps to keep all the steam inside, and a strip of sticky dough made of flour is laid around the neck of the pot in order to hold the lid in place and to ensure that no steam can escape. It is, however, possible to cook biryanis successfully in a standard cooking pot, preferably one made of heavy steel or copper. To seal the pot, well-moistened baking parchment can be used to cover the top layer of the rice, with a damp dish towel on top, and then a double thickness of foil.

Tawa Most unleavened breads such as chapatis are cooked on a cast-iron griddle known as a *tawa*. A bigger and heavier version of the domestic *tawa* is used by the street vendors in India to make tasty snacks, the aromas of which fill the air, drawing people towards the *tawa* like a magnet.

Tapeli Used for cooking rice, a *tapeli* is a useful pan made of heavy stainless steel or copper. A *tapeli* is shaped like a normal pan, but has a tight-fitting lid that is ideal for cooking rice by the absorption method.

Chapati rolling board This round wooden board on short stubby legs is used to mould breads into shape. The extra height provided by the legs helps to disperse excess dry flour. A wooden pastry board makes an appropriate substitute.

Chapati spoon The square, flat-headed chapati spoon is used for turning roasting breads on the hot chapati griddle. A fish slice (spatula) may also be used.

Colander and sieve (strainer) These are used for draining boiled rice and vegetables,

ABOVE The chapati rolling pin is available in many different sizes.

and for straining ingredients. Choose long-handled, sturdy varieties made from stainless steel, as these allow you to stand back to pour steaming rice out of a pan, and will not discolour like plastic ones.

Slotted spoon Stirring cooked, drained rice with a slotted spoon will make the rice soft and fluffy by allowing air to circulate between the grains. A slotted spoon is also useful for removing food from hot liquids.

Food processor Traditional grinding stones make the best chutneys and spice pastes, but a food processor is the answer for today's busy cooks. It can be used to chop and slice onions and make ginger and garlic purées, which are essential ingredients in Indian cooking. The purées can then be frozen in small quantities and used as and when required.

Masala dani A spice box, known as a *masala dani*, is the pride and joy of many an Indian cook. It is very often handed down from mother to daughter or grandmother to granddaughter. Small steel containers shaped like miniature cups are neatly arranged inside a large box with a lid, also made of stainless steel. The

ABOVE The *tawa* is a flat hot griddle pan traditionally used to cook chapatis on.

containers are used to store the whole spices, such as mustard seeds, cumin seeds, dried red chillies, nigella seeds and black pepper, that are used in everyday cooking.

Spice grinders In an ideal world, freshly ground spices are the only way to achieve full flavours, but modern life is so hectic that it is hard to find time to cook at all, never mind to grind the spices! However, whole spices do have a longer shelf-life than ground spices and can be ground in small quantities as and when required with the right equipment. In India, many households still use the traditional grinding stone (*sil-batta*), made of two stones: a flat platform on which the spices are placed, and a small cylindrical roller, rather like a rolling pin, used to grind spice pastes. A mortar and pestle (*haman-dasta*), is also traditionally used to grind dry spices. These methods do produce fabulous flavours, but electric gadgets such as coffee grinders are fast becoming the popular choice.

Tandoor Leavened breads such as naans of various kinds are cooked in the *tandoor*, a barrel-shaped clay oven. This was originally only used for cooking bread, but has now been adapted for all sorts of other dishes.

Cooking methods

The unique character of Indian cooking comes from the ingenious and skilful art of combining spices in various ways. Coupled with this are several basic techniques that let the cook create different flavours from the same range of spices.

Bhuna This is a method that involves frying the spices at a high temperature, but a small amount of water is added at regular intervals to stop them burning and sticking to the bottom of the pan. This enables the cook to scrape up the spices and mix them into the dish. It is this technique of scraping, stirring and mixing the spices without letting them burn that makes a perfect *bhuna* dish. Salt is added halfway through the cooking process to enable the food to release its natural juices, keeping the dish moist.

Dum This method of cooking is relatively easy. After the initial cooking process, the food is put into a heavy pan with a tight-fitting lid, and the pan is sealed completely so that no steam can escape. Traditionally, *dum* cooking is done over charcoal and live coals are placed on top of the lid after sealing it with a sticky dough made with plain (all-purpose) flour and water. It is crucial to follow the given cooking time because the pot is opened only when the food is fully cooked.

Korma The term *korma* is commonly misunderstood as meaning a dish, but it is in fact one of the most important techniques in Indian cooking. It simply means braising. There are different types of *kormas*. Northern *kormas* tend to be rich and creamy with subtle flavours and smooth, velvety sauces; nut pastes such as cashew and almond are used as well as cream and saffron. *Kormas* from south India are enriched with coconut milk and can be quite fiery. Whether they are pale and creamy or spicy and hot, the difference lies in the regional practice of combining and blending the ingredients. The size of the pan is very important in cooking a successful korma. If the pan is too big the food will dry out quickly; if too small it will produce too much juice. The pan should be just big enough to hold the main ingredients comfortably.

Tadka or baghar A heavy pan shaped like a miniature wok is used to heat up small amounts of oil, and the whole spices are then thrown into the hot oil, where they release their amazing aroma. Both the oil and the spices are then folded into the cooked dish. This technique is known as *tadka*, meaning 'seasoning'. In a western kitchen a steel ladle or a small pan is a perfect substitute utensil for preparing hot oil seasonings.

Talana This is a method of deep-frying that produces an exciting range of mouth-watering snacks. In India, a *kadhai*, which is shaped like a wok, is generally used for deep-frying. It is made of heavy cast iron and because of its shape, a small quantity of oil can be used. A few simple rules will ensure light and crispy deep-fried food. First, it is essential to use a light cooking oil such as sunflower oil. Second, the oil needs to be at the right temperature, usually about 80°C/350°F/Gas 4. A food thermometer is perfect for this, but a good way to judge the temperature without a thermometer is to drop in a small piece of bread as soon as the surface of the oil has a faint shimmer of rising smoke. The bread should rise to the surface in a few seconds without browning, and then turn brown in a minute or so.

Tandoori This is an age-old technique which is believed to have found its way into India with the ancient Persians.

ABOVE A perfect *bhuna* dish is made from a carefully fried combination of spices.

ABOVE The *tadka*, a small wok-like utensil, is used for warming oils and spices.

ABOVE The *korma* is an important cooking technique whereby ingredients are braised.

ABOVE In coastal regions of southern India, terracotta pots are favoured over metal pans.

ABOVE A pestle and mortar is ideal for grinding up fresh herbs and spices.

ABOVE Salt is always added during the cooking process rather than at the table.

A *tandoor* is a barrel-shaped clay oven that is capable of grilling (broiling), roasting and baking simultaneously. It is mainly used for cooking meat, poultry and leavened bread, although delectable vegetarian *tandoori* recipes have evolved with time. However, a domestic oven, grill (broiler) or barbecue can also produce tandoori-style food.

Cooking with salt and spices Using freshly ground spices for each meal is still common practice in India. However, it is possible to cook delicious food with pre-ground spices so long as they are stored away from direct light and used up quickly.

Using the correct amount of salt is vital. It is always added at the beginning or during

the cooking process, which ensures the proper blending of flavours. To some, the quantity used may seem excessive, but salt is treated almost as a spice, to balance all the flavours. In dry spiced vegetable recipes, salt is added at the very start, to help release the vegetable juices and preserve all the nutrients.

Using Spices

Mastering the art of maintaining a delicate balance of spices comes with practice and care. To produce a really great dish, bear the following important points in mind.

- Using freshly ground spices for each meal produces the most fabulous flavours.
- The sequence in which the chosen spices are added affects the final taste of the dish.
- Cooking the spices is the most important step in creating a good curry.
- It is essential to fry the spices at different temperatures in order to achieve a rounded flavour, so follow the timings and temperatures specified in a recipe.
- Dry spices, ground or whole, should be gently sizzled over a very low heat so that they do not burn.
- Wet spices such as onion, ginger and garlic should be fried over gentle heat and allowed to become soft and translucent before adding the other ingredients.

north india

North Indian food was greatly influenced by foreign invaders, and the presence of royal households in this area led to the creation of many luxurious vegetarian dishes. Exotic Lotus Root Kebabs, Chickpeas in a Spice-laced Yogurt Sauce, rich Lentils with Spiced Butter, and fragrant basmati rice cooked with evocative saffron are some of the fine examples. There are also simple vegetarian dishes that are used during religious festivals and for everyday meals.

Flavours of the north

Comprising four states – Jammu and Kashmir, Himachal Pradesh, the Punjab and Uttar Pradesh – north India stretches from the mountainous north-west to the valley of the river Brahmaputra in the east. It is not surprising that such a diverse range of flavours and cuisine should have evolved from such a vast and varied region.

Kashmir's most prized possession is saffron and the best quality saffron in the world is grown here. Summertime transforms Kashmir into a colourful patchwork of fruits, vegetables and flowers, and the lakes are occupied by floating fruit and vegetable markets attracting thousands of people. Tomatoes, watermelons, cucumbers, sweet, juicy plums and peaches, rich red cherries, almonds and walnuts all thrive in the cool mountain climate.

Kashmiri cuisine offers some of the most exquisite-tasting vegetable dishes. It uses ingredients such as the delectable morel mushroom, the roots of locally grown lotus flowers, walnuts, dried dates and apricots, to create a wide range of exotic meals. The nearest northern neighbour to Kashmir is Himachal Pradesh, popularly known as the 'mountain state'. Cooking here is very similar to that of Kashmir, with locally grown fruits, vegetables and spices. Dishes such as sweet stuffed green and red (bell) peppers and chickpeas cooked in an aromatic yogurt sauce are very popular.

Tandoori cooking, which originated in the Punjab, uses both meat and vegetables and is popular all over the country. Spicy mustard greens (sarson ka saag), accompanied by griddle baked cornmeal bread (makki ki roti) mark the winter harvest festival in the state. In the summer copious amounts of lassi (a cooling yogurt drink) is drunk.

The capital city of Delhi is truly a food lover's paradise. Its cuisine is both rich and varied and most is of Mogul origin. Saffron-scented kormas and pasandas, with silky smooth sauces and rich tastes, are popular throughout India. Richly flavoured soups (shorbas) and desserts such as kulfi are some of the fine examples of Mogul-influenced dishes.

Uttar Pradesh produces rice, wheat, barley, maize and sugarcane. Basmati rice, which is grown in the Dehra Dun area, is one of the best in the country. The famous Awadhi cuisine, predominant in the area, is reminiscent of the bygone days of the royal kitchens.

The influence of Awadhi cuisine is very strong in the city of Lucknow, the capital of Uttar Pradesh. Rich ingredients and elaborate cooking methods are what differentiate Awadhi cuisine from the rest of the sub-continent. The *dum* (steam cooking) style of cooking originated here, and a typical banqueting table in the royal household would consist of elaborate biryanis, luxurious kormas, melt-in-the-mouth kebabs, and rich, saffron-scented flaky bread.

The following pages will introduce you to a wealth of north-Indian colours and flavours, so start cooking to sample a wealth of culinary delights.

Lotus Root Kebabs

Nadhru Kababs

In the Hindu religion, the strikingly beautiful lotus flower is synonymous with spiritual awakening. In this Kashmiri recipe, exotic lotus flower roots are lightly mashed and blended with potatoes and spices and then shaped into flat cakes, as enticing as they are delectable. Fresh lotus roots are highly nutritious but are difficult to obtain. However, canned and vacuum-packed lotus roots are available from Asian grocery stores. The canned roots are a pale creamy colour because they are bleached as part of the canning process. They should be drained and rinsed well before use. When buying the vacuum-packed varieties, you should look for orange-coloured ones, as this is the natural colour of lotus roots.

1 Blend the lotus roots and potatoes in a food processor; the potatoes should be smooth, but the lotus roots should still have a rough texture. Transfer the mixture to a mixing bowl.

2 Heat the oil over a medium heat and fry the onion, ginger, green and red chillies for 3–4 minutes until the onion is soft. Add the fried mixture to the lotus root and potato mix and stir in the fennel seeds, garam masala, salt and coriander leaves. Mix well, then chill the mixture for 35–40 minutes.

3 Divide the mixture into 12 equal parts and make flat cakes 1cm/½in thick. Dip each cake in the beaten egg and roll in the poppy seeds.

4 Heat the oil in a frying pan over a medium heat and fry the kebabs for about 2 minutes on each side. Drain on kitchen paper and serve with Almond Chutney.

Makes 12

400g/14oz canned lotus roots, drained and well rinsed

350g/12oz boiled potatoes

30ml/2 tbsp sunflower oil or plain olive oil

1 small onion, finely chopped

1cm/½in piece of fresh root ginger, grated

1 fresh green chilli, finely chopped (seeded if you like)

1 fresh red chilli, finely chopped (seeded if you like)

2.5ml/½ tsp fennel seeds

5ml/1 tsp garam masala

3.5ml/¾ tsp salt or to taste

30ml/2 tbsp coriander (cilantro) leaves, finely chopped

1 egg, beaten

75g/3oz white poppy seeds

Oil for shallow frying

Cook's Tip

Jerusalem artichokes are a good alternative – you will need about 250g/9oz for this recipe.

PER PORTION Energy 118kcal/491kJ; Protein 2.4g; Carbohydrate 5.5g, of which sugars 1g; Fat 9.8g, of which saturates 1.3g; Cholesterol 16mg; Calcium 63mg; Fibre 1.3g; Sodium 32mg.

Stuffed Sweet Peppers

Bharwan Shimla Mirch

Sweet peppers are grown extensively in the hilly terrain of Kashmir and Shimla, and in India they are known as pahadi mirch, meaning 'mountain chillies'. In this recipe, the peppers are stuffed with a mixture of crushed boiled potatoes, cashew nuts and spices. Green peppers are used, but for a more colourful dish, you can also use red and yellow ones, which will vary the taste.

1 Boil the potatoes in their skins (this is important as the potatoes, when mashed, should not be mushy), then cool and peel them. Crush them lightly with a fork so that some larger pieces remain.

2 Heat 3 tbsp of the oil in a frying pan over a medium heat, and when it is quite hot, but not smoking, throw in the mustard seeds, followed by the cumin seeds. Let the seeds pop for 10–15 seconds, then add the onion and green chilli. Fry, stirring regularly, for 5–6 minutes until the onion is soft.

3 Add the turmeric, chilli powder, garam masala and cashew nuts to the pan, cook for about a minute and remove from the heat. Add this mixture to the mashed potato, and stir in the salt, coriander leaves and lemon juice. Mix thoroughly and set aside.

4 Pre-heat the oven to 190°C/375°F/Gas 5.

5 Wash the peppers and slice off the tops. Using a small knife, carefully remove the white pith and the seeds. Fill the peppers with the spiced potato mixture right to the top, pressing the filling down into the cavity. Smooth the surface with a knife or the back of a spoon.

6 Heat the remaining 30ml/2 tbsp oil over a medium heat and add the filled peppers to the pan. Stir them around until the peppers are fully coated with the oil. Stand the peppers in an ovenproof dish or roasting pan, and bake them in the centre of the oven for 25–30 minutes, turning and basting them occasionally. Serve with Roasted Tomato Chutney.

Serves 4–6

275g/10oz potatoes
75ml/5 tbsp sunflower oil or plain olive oil
2.5ml/½ tsp black mustard seeds
2.5ml/½ tsp cumin seeds
1 large onion, finely chopped
1 green chilli, finely chopped (seeded if you like)
2.5ml/½ tsp ground turmeric
2.5ml/½ tsp chilli powder
5ml/1 tsp garam masala
50g/2oz/½ cup raw cashew nuts, chopped
5ml/1 tsp salt or to taste
30ml/2 tbsp coriander (cilantro) leaves, finely chopped
15ml/1 tbsp lemon juice
4 medium-sized green (bell) peppers

PER PORTION Energy 224kcal/933kJ; Protein 4.6g; Carbohydrate 20.2g, of which sugars 10.1g; Fat 14.5g, of which saturates 2.2g; Cholesterol 0mg; Calcium 29mg; Fibre 3.1g; Sodium 36mg.

Spiced Corn on the Cob

Bhutte Masala

Corn on the cob, roasted over live charcoal, fills the air with delicious aromas in the streets of north India. The street vendors brush the cobs with melted butter and sprinkle them with black salt, chillies and other spices. In India, fresh corn is used, but you can use frozen if you wish – just make sure you thaw the cobs slightly before slicing them.

1 Slice the corn cobs into 1cm/½in circles and put the slices into a roomy pan. Add the coconut milk, chillies and salt. Pour in 100ml/3½fl oz/⅓ cup water and bring the mixture to the boil. Reduce the heat to low, cover and simmer for 10 minutes, stirring halfway through the cooking time.

2 Just before the end of the cooking time, heat the oil in a small pan over a medium heat. When it is hot, but not smoking, add the mustard seeds, followed by the cumin seeds. Let them pop for 5–10 seconds and then pour the contents of the pan over the corn.

3 Add the green chillies, fresh coriander and lemon juice. Stir, uncovered, until all the liquid evaporates and the coconut sauce coats the corn. Remove from the heat and serve.

Serves 4

4 corn on the cob, fresh or frozen

150ml/5fl oz/½ cup coconut milk

2 dried red chillies, chopped

5ml/1 tsp salt or to taste

30ml/2 tbsp sunflower oil or plain olive oil

2.5ml/½ tsp black mustard seeds

2.5ml/½ tsp cumin seeds

2 green chillies, seeded and chopped

15ml/1 tbsp coriander (cilantro) leaves, finely chopped

25ml/1½ tbsp lemon juice

PER PORTION Energy 164kcal/689kJ; Protein 4.2g; Carbohydrate 20.1g, of which sugars 4g; Fat 8g, of which saturates 1.1g; Cholesterol 0mg; Calcium 19mg; Fibre 2g; Sodium 44mg.

Serves 4

300g/10oz/1¼ cups full-fat (whole)
   natural (plain) yogurt
10ml/2 tsp gram flour
50g/2oz/4 tbsp ghee
1.5ml/¼ tsp asafoetida
2.5cm/1in piece cinnamon stick
4 green cardamom pods, bruised
2 brown cardamom pods, bruised
4 cloves
2.5ml/½ tsp black pepper, crushed
5ml/1 tsp ground cumin
2.5ml/½ tsp ground turmeric
5ml/1 tsp ginger purée
600g/1¼lb/4 cups canned chickpeas,
   drained and rinsed
5ml/1 tsp salt or to taste
3.5ml/¾ tsp sugar
2.5ml/½ tsp garam masala

To garnish:
Sprigs of fresh mint

PER PORTION Energy 367kcal/1540kJ; Protein 15.9g; Carbohydrate 34.3g, of which sugars 7.5g; Fat 19.6g, of which saturates 7.7g; Cholesterol 8mg; Calcium 225mg; Fibre 6.2g; Sodium 392mg.

Chickpeas in a Spice-laced Yogurt Sauce
Channa Madra

The people of the Himalayan state of Himachal Pradesh are predominantly meat-eaters, but they also have some delicious vegetarian dishes, and this is one of the most popular. Chickpeas are simmered in yogurt infused with cardamom and cloves, producing a beautifully fragrant sauce. This recipe uses ghee, which does lend a distinctive, rich taste, but sunflower oil or plain olive oil would work instead.

1 Whisk the yogurt and gram flour together and set aside.

2 Melt the ghee over a low heat and add the asafoetida, followed by the cinnamon, both types of cardamom pods, cloves, black pepper, cumin, turmeric and ginger. Stir-fry for 30 seconds and add the yogurt. Increase the heat slightly and cook, stirring regularly, for 4–5 minutes.

3 Add the chickpeas, salt and sugar. Cover the pan and reduce the heat to low. Simmer for 10–12 minutes, then stir in the garam masala and remove from the heat. Transfer to a serving dish and garnish with the fresh mint. Serve with chapatis or phulkas.

Serves 4

60ml/4 tbsp sunflower oil or plain olive oil

10ml/2 tsp ginger purée

10ml/2 tsp garlic purée

1 large onion, finely sliced

5ml/1 tsp ground cumin

5ml/1 tsp ground coriander

2.5ml/½ tsp ground turmeric

5ml/1 tsp chilli powder

125g/4 oz canned chopped tomatoes with
    their juice

400g/14oz/3 cups canned chickpeas,
    drained and rinsed

175g/6oz boiled potatoes, cut into
    2.5cm/1in cubes

5ml/1 tsp salt or to taste

5ml/1 tsp sun-dried mango powder
    (amchur) or 25ml/1½ tbsp lemon juice

2.5ml/½ tsp garam masala

15ml/1 tbsp coriander (cilantro) leaves,
    finely chopped

15ml/1 tbsp fresh mint leaves, chopped

To garnish:

1 small tomato, seeded and cut
    into julienne strips

1 small onion, coarsely chopped

1 green chilli, seeded and cut into
    julienne strips

Sprigs of fresh mint

PER PORTION Energy 300kcal/1256kJ; Protein 10.1g;
Carbohydrate 33.7g, of which sugars 7.5g; Fat 15g, of
which saturates 1.8g; Cholesterol 0mg; Calcium 82mg;
Fibre 6.2g; Sodium 232mg.

Spiced Chickpeas with Cumin, Coriander, Chilli and Lime

Chole

The people of Punjab have mastered the art of cooking chickpeas and combining them with a fragrant mixture of spices. This dish is a true delight and, served garnished with tomato, raw onion, green chilli and mint, makes a sumptuous meal.

1 Heat the oil over a low heat in a heavy pan and add the ginger and garlic; stir-fry for 30 seconds.

2 Add the sliced onion, increase the heat to medium and fry for 6–7 minutes or until the onion is soft and just beginning to colour. Add the cumin, coriander, turmeric and chilli powder and stir-fry for 1 minute, then add the tomatoes. Cook for 3–4 minutes or until the oil begins to separate from the spiced tomato mixture.

3 Add the chickpeas, potatoes, salt and 150ml/5fl oz/½ cup warm water. Bring it to the boil and reduce the heat to low. Cover the pan and simmer for 10–12 minutes. Blend the sun-dried mango powder with a little water and add to the chickpeas, or add the lemon juice.

4 Stir in the garam masala, coriander and mint leaves and remove the pan from the heat. Transfer to a serving dish and garnish with the ingredients listed above. Serve with bhature (deep-fried leavened bread) or any other bread.

Lentils with Spiced Butter

Dhal Makhani

North India's most famous lentil dish, dhal makhani, is made with black lentils, known as urad dhal. They are available in Indian stores and some large supermarkets. If you cannot get urad dhal, try channa dhal instead. This will produce a completely different taste, but makes a delicious dish all the same. No north Indian wedding banquet or special occasion meal is complete without dhal makhani.

1 Wash the lentils in several changes of water and soak them for 3–4 hours, or overnight. Drain well and put them into a heavy pan with 600ml/1 pint/2½ cups water.

2 Bring to the boil, then add the garlic, ginger, chilli powder and whole green chillies. Reduce the heat to low, cover and simmer for 25–30 minutes. Mash about a quarter of the lentils with the back of a spoon in the pan.

3 Add the kidney beans, tomato purée, fresh tomatoes, salt and sugar. Cover and simmer for 5–6 minutes. Add the butter and cream, and simmer gently for a further 5 minutes.

4 Remove from the heat and serve, garnished with the julienne strips of ginger and fresh tomato, and accompanied by naan or phulka bread or chapatis.

Serves 4

175g/6oz/¾ cup whole black lentils
   (urad dhal)
10ml/2 tsp garlic purée
10ml/2 tsp ginger purée
2.5–5ml/½–1 tsp chilli powder
2–3 whole fresh green chillies
50g/2oz/⅓ cup canned red kidney beans,
   drained and rinsed
30ml/2 tbsp tomato purée (paste)
150g/5oz fresh tomatoes, skinned
   and chopped
5ml/1 tsp salt or to taste
2.5ml/½ tsp sugar
50g/2oz/4 tbsp butter
150ml/5fl oz/½ cup double (heavy) cream

To garnish:
Fine julienne strips of fresh root ginger and
   fresh tomato

PER PORTION Energy 420kcal/1750kJ; Protein 13g; Carbohydrate 27.9g, of which sugars 4.9g; Fat 31.4g, of which saturates 18.1g; Cholesterol 78mg; Calcium 71mg; Fibre 5.5g; Sodium 184mg.

Royal Corn Curry

Shahi Bhutta

Corn is an extremely popular vegetable in northern India, where the cornfields of Punjab make a wonderful sight as the crops sway in the breeze. In India, the corn kernels for this dish would be meticulously removed from the cob just before preparing the dish, but ready frozen or canned kernels save time and work equally well.

1 Grind the poppy seeds, coconut and coriander seeds in a coffee grinder until fine and set aside.

2 Heat the oil in a frying pan over a low heat and fry the cardamom pods gently for 25–30 seconds until they puff up, then increase the heat to medium and add the onion, ginger and chillies. Fry for 8–9 minutes, until the onion is lightly browned, stirring frequently to encourage even browning.

3 Add the turmeric and the ground ingredients. Cook for a further minute and then add the corn, milk and salt. Let the mixture simmer gently for 8–10 minutes or until the sauce has thickened, stirring occasionally.

4 Add the tomatoes and garam masala and transfer the mixture to a serving dish. Serve with any bread and/or Saffron-scented Pilau Rice.

Serves 4

15ml/1 tbsp white poppy seeds

15ml/1 tbsp desiccated (dry unsweetened shredded) coconut

5ml/1 tsp coriander seeds

60ml/4 tbsp sunflower oil or plain olive oil

4 green cardamom pods, bruised

1 large onion, finely chopped

10ml/2 tsp ginger purée

2 green chillies, finely chopped (seeded if you like)

2.5ml/½ tsp ground turmeric

450g/1lb/2½ cups frozen corn, thawed and drained, or canned corn, drained and well rinsed

225ml/8fl oz/scant 1 cup full-fat (whole) milk

5ml/1 tsp salt or to taste

110g/4oz fresh tomatoes, skinned and chopped

2.5ml/½ tsp garam masala

PER PORTION Energy 368kcal/1539kJ; Protein 7.7g; Carbohydrate 43.6g, of which sugars 21.6g; Fat 19.4g, of which saturates 5.2g; Cholesterol 8mg; Calcium 128mg; Fibre 4.4g; Sodium 343mg.

Serves 4

60ml/4 tbsp mustard oil

700g/1½lb small potatoes, boiled and peeled

2.5–5ml/½–1 tsp chilli powder

2 brown cardamom pods, bruised

4 green cardamom pods, bruised

2.5ml/½ tsp ground ginger

5ml/1 tsp ground coriander

5ml/1 tsp ground fennel

5ml/1 tsp salt or to taste

150g/5oz/½ cup natural (plain) yogurt, whisked

PER PORTION Energy 261kcal/1092kJ; Protein 5.8g; Carbohydrate 33.2g, of which sugars 5.1g; Fat 12.7g, of which saturates 1.8g; Cholesterol 1mg; Calcium 93mg; Fibre 1.8g; Sodium 53mg.

Potatoes in Aromatic Yogurt Sauce

Dum Aloo Kashmiri

In Indian cooking, the humble potato is given gourmet status in many different dishes, and this is one of the most delicious. Here whole potatoes (small new potatoes are excellent for this dish) are fried before being simmered in a yogurt sauce. The people of Kashmir cook these potatoes in mustard oil, which does add a very special flavour, and needs to be heated until smoking hot to reduce its pungency and give the dish a superbly nutty, mellow flavour.

1 In a medium-sized pan, heat the oil until smoking and fry the potatoes in two batches until they are well browned. Take the pan off the heat and drain the potatoes on kitchen paper. When they are cool enough to handle, prick the potatoes all over to allow the flavours to penetrate.

2 Place the pan back over a low heat and add the chilli powder, followed by 30ml/2 tbsp water. Cook for 1 minute and add all the remaining spices. Cook for a further minute.

3 Add the browned potatoes, salt and yogurt. Cover the pan tightly and reduce the heat to low. Cook until the sauce thickens and coats the potatoes (5–6 minutes). Remove from the heat and serve with naan bread or chapatis.

Saffron-scented Pilau Rice

Kesar Pulao

Pilau rice, sometimes studded with dried fruits such as apricots and raisins, is a delicacy enjoyed in the hilly terrain of northern India. This is a basic recipe for spicy saffron-scented rice, which provides a delicate accompaniment to so many main dishes. Using this recipe as the basis, you can create a whole array of different types of pilau. Add stir-fried cubes of paneer (Indian cheese) and garden peas to make a splendid meal that will provide carbohydrate, protein and vitamins in one dish. Canned and rinsed chickpeas tossed in garlic and ginger will create a nutritious and delicious chickpea pilau. You can also vary the garnish by using fried onion.

1 Wash the rice in several changes of water and leave it to soak in cold water for up to 20 minutes.

2 Soak the pounded saffron in the hot milk and set aside.

3 In a heavy pan, melt the ghee or butter gently over a low heat and add the cardamom, cinnamon, cloves and star anise. Allow them to sizzle for 25–30 seconds.

4 Drain the rice and add to the spiced butter. Add the salt and stir to mix well, then pour in 450ml/16fl oz/2 cups hot water and bring to the boil. Let it boil for a minute or two and reduce the heat to low, cover the pan and cook for 7–8 minutes. Remove from the heat, sprinkle the saffron-infused milk and the rose water over the top, then cover the pan again and let it stand for 10 minutes.

5 Fluff up the rice with a fork, and, using a metal spoon, transfer it to a serving dish and garnish with the toasted almonds. Serve with chapatis or phulka bread.

Serves 4

225g/8oz/1 cup basmati rice

Good pinch of saffron threads, pounded

30ml/2 tbsp hot milk

25g/1oz/4 tbsp ghee or unsalted butter

4 green cardamom pods, bruised

2.5cm/1in piece of cinnamon stick

4 cloves

2 star anise

2.5ml/½ tsp salt

25ml/1½ tbsp rose water

To garnish:

Toasted almonds

PER PORTION Energy 262kcal/1090kJ; Protein 4.4g; Carbohydrate 45.3g, of which sugars 0.4g; Fat 6.7g, of which saturates 3g; Cholesterol 0mg; Calcium 20mg; Fibre 0g; Sodium 4mg.

Griddle-roasted Wholemeal Flat Breads
Chapati and Phulka

Flat breads are a great accompaniment to vegetarian dishes. They can be served with chutneys and pickles or as part of a main meal. Chapatis are dry-roasted on an iron griddle (*tawa*). The dough can also be used to make phulkas, which puff up like balloons under the grill and are delicious spread with a little melted butter.

Makes 16

400g/14oz/3½ cups chapati flour (atta) or
    fine wholemeal (whole-wheat) flour
5ml/1 tsp salt
250ml/8fl oz/1 cup water
A little extra flour for dusting

1 Mix the flour and salt together in a mixing bowl. Gradually add the water, continuing to mix until a dough is formed. Transfer the dough to a flat surface and knead it for 4–5 minutes. When all the excess moisture is absorbed by the flour, wrap the dough in clear film (plastic wrap) and let it rest for 30 minutes. Alternatively, make the dough in a food processor.

2 Divide the dough into 2 equal parts and pinch or cut 8 equal portions from each. Form the portions into balls and flatten them into neat, round cakes. Dust the cakes lightly in the flour and roll each one out to a 15cm/6in circle. Keep the rest of the cakes covered with a damp cloth.

3 For chapatis: pre-heat a heavy cast-iron griddle over a medium/high heat. Place a dough circle on it, cook for about 30 seconds and turn it over, using a thin metal spatula. Cook until bubbles begin to appear on the surface and turn it over again. Press the edges down gently with a clean cloth to encourage the chapati to puff up (they will not always puff up, but this does not affect the taste). Cook until the underneath begins to brown. Keep cooked chapatis hot by wrapping them in foil lined with kitchen paper.

4 For phulkas: pre-heat the grill (broiler) to high, and also pre-heat a heavy griddle as above. Place a dough circle on the griddle over a medium/high heat. Cook for 35–40 seconds and then immediately place it under the grill, uncooked side up, about 13cm/5in below the heat source. Let the phulka puff up until brown spots appear on the surface. Watch it carefully as this happens quite quickly. Remove and place the phulka on a piece of foil lined with kitchen paper.

PER PORTION Energy 78kcal/330kJ; Protein 3.2g; Carbohydrate 16g, of which sugars 0.5g; Fat 0.6g, of which saturates 0.1g; Cholesterol 0mg; Calcium 10mg; Fibre 2.3g; Sodium 124mg.

Makes 8

350g/12oz/3 cups plain (all-purpose) flour
plus extra for dusting

2.5ml/½ tsp salt

2.5ml/½ tsp sugar

5ml/1 tsp baking powder

150g/5oz/generous ½ cup natural
(plain) yogurt

1 egg

30–45ml/2–3 tbsp warm water

Oil for deep frying

PER PORTION Energy 244kcal/1027kJ; Protein 5.9g;
Carbohydrate 35.7g, of which sugars 2.4g; Fat 9.7g, of
which saturates 1.2g; Cholesterol 24mg; Calcium 101mg;
Fibre 1.4g; Sodium 149mg.

Deep-fried Leavened Bread

Bhature

Bhature served with spiced chickpeas is a Punjabi speciality. The dough for the bhature is made with yogurt and a little water, which results in a soft and luscious bread. Serve with any type of curry.

1 Put the flour, salt, sugar and baking powder into a large mixing bowl and mix well.

2 Beat the yogurt and egg together and add to the flour along with the warm water. Mix until a dough has formed, then transfer it to a flat surface. Knead it for 4–5 minutes until the dough is soft and pliable. Alternatively, make the dough in the food processor. Place it in a plastic food bag and leave to rest in a warm place for 2–3 hours.

3 Divide the dough into 8 equal parts and form each one into a ball, then flatten to a smooth, round cake. Dust each cake lightly in the flour and roll it out to a circle about 13cm/5in across.

4 Heat the oil in a wok or other suitable pan for deep-frying over a medium heat. Check that the temperature is right by dropping a tiny amount of the dough into the hot oil. If the dough floats to the surface immediately without turning brown, then the temperature is just right. Alternatively, use a thermometer and check the oil has reached at least 180°C (350°F).

5 Place a dough cake in the hot oil and fry for about a minute. When it puffs up, turn it over and fry the other side for another minute or until browned. Drain on kitchen paper. Serve with Spiced Chickpeas with Cumin, Coriander, Chilli and Lime, or any other curry.

Almond Chutney

Badam Ki Chutney

Almonds are very popular throughout northern India, where beautiful almond blossoms appear in the orchards of Kashmir at the onset of spring. In Indian cooking, fresh chutneys such as this tasty almond one are made by simply grinding all the ingredients to a smooth purée. This chutney recipe can also be made by substituting the almonds with the same quantity of desiccated coconut instead.

1 Soak the almonds in 175ml/6fl oz/¾ cup boiling water for 15 minutes.

2 Put them in a blender, with the water in which they were soaked. Add the remaining ingredients and blend until smooth.

3 Transfer to a glass serving bowl and chill. Serve with fried and grilled (broiled) snacks or use as a dip with poppadums.

Serves 4–5

50g/2oz/½ cup blanched almonds

1 green chilli, roughly chopped (seeded if you like)

1 small clove garlic

1cm/½in piece of fresh root ginger, roughly chopped

15g/½oz coriander (cilantro) leaves and stalks

30ml/2 tbsp fresh mint leaves

2.5ml/½ tsp salt

5ml/1 tsp sugar

15ml/1 tbsp lemon juice

PER PORTION Energy 79kcal/330kJ; Protein 3.1g; Carbohydrate 3.4g, of which sugars 1.3g; Fat 6.1g, of which saturates 0.5g; Cholesterol 0mg; Calcium 61mg; Fibre 0.7g; Sodium 201mg.

Spice-infused Kashmiri Tea
Qahwa

Spiced tea is enjoyed all over India, but the difference lies in the regional variation of the spices. Drinking spiced tea is a Kashmiri tradition. During the freezing winters in this Himalayan region, spiced tea is brewed throughout the day. The spices used, such as cinnamon, cardamom and cloves, are known to induce body heat and this is one of the ways by which Kashmiris keep themselves warm.

1 Bring the water to the boil in a pan and add all the spices. Simmer for 5 minutes.

2 Rinse out a teapot with boiling water and put in the leaf tea or tea bags. Pour over the spiced water along with all the whole spices.

3 Brew the tea for 5 minutes and strain into individual cups. Add milk and sugar if you like, but it is also delicious without milk.

Serves 2

450ml/16fl oz/2 cups water

1cm/½in piece of cinnamon stick

2 green cardamom pods, bruised

2 cloves

A small pinch (about 8 threads) of saffron, pounded

15ml/1 tbsp leaf tea or 2 tea bags

Milk and sugar to taste

PER PORTION Energy 15kcal/66kJ; Protein 1g; Carbohydrate 1.8g, of which sugars 0g; Fat 0.7g, of which saturates 0.1g; Cholesterol 0mg; Calcium 9mg; Fibre 0g; Sodium 2mg.

Serves 4–5

A pinch of saffron threads, pounded

15ml/1 tbsp hot milk

300ml/10fl oz/1¼ cups full-fat (whole) milk

50g/2oz/⅓ cup ground rice

400ml/14fl oz/1½ cups canned evaporated milk

50g/2oz/¼ cup granulated (white) sugar

25g/1oz/¼ cup blanched, flaked (sliced) almonds

25g/1oz/¼ cup pistachio nuts

5ml/1 tsp ground cardamom

15ml/1 tbsp rose water

To garnish:

2–3 dried ready-to-eat apricots, sliced

PER PORTION Energy 262kcal/1096kJ; Protein 11.1g; Carbohydrate 30.2g, of which sugars 22g; Fat 11.3g, of which saturates 3.9g; Cholesterol 22mg; Calcium 308mg; Fibre 0.7g; Sodium 127mg.

Ground Rice in Saffron-scented Milk

Phirni

This is a luxurious dessert in which a small quantity of ground rice is cooked in a large volume of milk with saffron and spices until it is reduced to the consistency of evaporated milk. In Kashmir this dessert is set in earthenware bowls, which are specially treated so that the mixture can be left to set without losing any liquid. Stemmed glasses or glazed ramekins work just as well.

1 Soak the saffron threads in the hot milk and set aside.

2 Brush the surface of a heavy pan with a little oil to prevent the milk sticking to the bottom of the pan, then pour in the full-fat milk. Sprinkle the ground rice evenly over the milk and place the pan over a medium heat. Bring it to the boil, stirring frequently.

3 Add the evaporated milk, sugar and almonds. Reserve a few pistachio nuts and add the remainder to the milk. Continue to cook over a low heat, stirring frequently, until the mixture thickens and resembles the consistency of cooked custard.

4 Stir in the ground cardamom and rose water and remove from the heat. Transfer to stemmed glasses or ramekins. Crush the reserved pistachio nuts and sprinkle over the top with the sliced apricots. Chill the dessert for at least 2 hours before serving.

north-east india

The people of the north-eastern region of India use locally grown vegetables, especially the leafy variety, to prepare numerous types of flavoursome and extremely healthy dishes. From Spiced Yam Fingers, Garlic-flavoured Mung Beans with Courgettes, and Duck Eggs with Cauliflower to Cardamom-scented Coconut Dumplings and Black Sesame Seed Fudge, the region offers a fabulous variety of sensational tastes and flavours.

Flavours of north-east India

With emerald-green mountains, meandering rivers, stunning lakes, lush tea plantations and acres of paddy fields, the north-east is one of the most beautiful parts of India. Comprising seven states, it is the largest region in the country. With the majestic Himalayan range of mountains spreading across the north-eastern border of the country, this region is heavily influenced by the mountain states such as Nepal and Bhutan. Among the seven states, Assam is the largest. The culture and civilization of Assam evolved around foreign powers such as the Dravidians, Aryans, Alpines, Tibetans, Burmese and the Indo-Mongolians. The intermingling of these cultures is what gave rise to the unique and unusual community known today as the Assamese. The state of Assam is well known for its highly prized tea and exquisite silks, and also produces large crops of rice and turmeric.

The daily Assamese diet is simple and nutritious. The emphasis is on fresh greens and locally grown vegetables such as yam, bitter gourd, milk gourd and sweet potatoes. Fragrant greens, grown only in this area, add plenty of flavours to vegetarian food. One of the greens, cooked like spinach and known as mani-muni sak, has been found to have important medicinal properties. The food of Assam is similar to that of its neighbouring state Bengal. As in Bengal, Assamese food is also cooked in mustard oil and the use of panchphoron, a creation of the Bengali cooks, is widely prevalent. There is a huge selection of typical vegetarian dishes such as khar, which is made using different types of vegetables, lentils and peas. Raw papaya is the most popular vegetable used in a khar, which is made with an ingredient typical to the state, known as kharoni. Kharoni is made from the burnt-down ashes of the banana trunk, which is known to aid digestion. Tenga, a lemon and tomato curry, is a popular dish which can be made with either fresh vegetables or lentils. The climate in Assam is temperate and fruits such as pinapple, plum, peach and star fruit grow in abundance.

Among the other six smaller states, Arunachal Pradesh, meaning 'land of the dawn-lit mountains' and Meghalaya are considered to be the most stunning. As Arunachal Pradesh is situated directly in the shadow of the mighty Himalayas, snow-clad peaks, crystal clear rivers and thick alpine forests are some of the wonderful features that contribute to this state's serene natural beauty. Local fruit and vegetables play an important part in the diet of the people of this state. Meghalaya, meaning 'abode of the clouds', also in the foothills of the Himalayas, is surrounded by breathtaking scenery. Fruits, vegetables and spices are grown locally, and Meghalaya turmeric is one of India's most prized spices.

In the small states of Manipur, Tripura, Nagaland and Mizoram, pulses and rice are the staples and vegetables are eaten every day along with fish and meat, which are cooked in mustard oil. Tripura, Nagaland and Mizoram are landlocked states and they rely mainly on locally grown produce. The food in Tripura has a striking resemblance to that of Bengali cuisine. Nagaland borders the states of Assam and Arunachal Pradesh and Myanmar, and the food is simply cooked with ginger, garlic and chillies. Smoked food is highly popular in this region.

Fresh Vegetables in Chilli, Ginger and Garlic Broth

Oying

This dish originates from the scenic mountain state of Arunachal Pradesh. The cuisine of this region is simple, delicious and extremely nutritious. Most of the cooking is done without using any fat, as in this recipe, relying instead on the use of fresh herbs and spices to give it its superb, distinct flavours.

1 Put the potatoes in a medium-sized pan, pour in 750ml/1¼ pints/3 cups water and bring it to the boil. Add the chillies, reduce the heat to low, cover and cook for 7–8 minutes.

2 Add the green beans and cabbage, bring back to the boil, cover and cook over a medium heat for 5 minutes. Add the salt, ginger and garlic, put the lid back on the pan and continue to cook for another 5 minutes.

3 Stir in the spinach and cook for a further 1–2 minutes until it has wilted. Add the coriander leaves, cook for about 1 minute, then remove from the heat and serve with hot crusty rolls.

Serves 4

250g/9oz/1 cup potatoes, cut into
   2.5cm/1in cubes

1–2 green chillies, sliced diagonally (seeded
   if you like)

150g/5oz/1 cup green beans, cut into
   2.5cm/1in lengths

150g/5oz/1 cup green cabbage,
   coarsely chopped

5ml/1 tsp salt or to taste

10ml/2 tsp grated fresh root ginger

1 large garlic clove, crushed

150g/5oz/1 cup fresh spinach,
   roughly chopped

15–30ml/1–2 tbsp coriander (cilantro)
   leaves, chopped

PER PORTION Energy 77kcal/322kJ; Protein 3.7g;
Carbohydrate 14.1g, of which sugars 4.4g; Fat 0.9g, of
which saturates 0.2g; Cholesterol 0mg; Calcium 125mg;
Fibre 3.7g; Sodium 66mg.

Serves 4

450g/1lb yam

45ml/3 tbsp sunflower oil or plain olive oil

10ml/2 tsp garlic purée

2.5–5ml/½–1 tsp chilli powder

2.5ml/½ tsp ground turmeric

5ml/1 tsp salt or to taste

PER PORTION Energy 209kcal/880kJ; Protein 2.2g;
Carbohydrate 32.8g, of which sugars 0.9g; Fat 8.6g, of
which saturates 1.1g; Cholesterol 0mg; Calcium 18mg;
Fibre 1.7g; Sodium 3mg.

Spiced Yam Fingers

Kath Alu Bhoja

These deliciously crispy yam bites are rather like French fries with a
spicy coating, and are often served at informal parties. They are
easy to make and very tasty. Yams are readily available in larger
supermarkets, as well as in Asian and African stores.

1 Peel and cut the yam into thin fingers to resemble French fries. Wash and dry thoroughly
with a cloth.

2 In a large frying pan, heat the oil over a low heat. Add the garlic and fry gently until it is
light brown.

3 Add the chilli powder, turmeric, salt and yam fingers, and stir over a medium heat for
2–3 minutes. Reduce the heat slightly, cover the pan and cook for 8–9 minutes until the
yam is tender.

4 Remove the lid and increase the heat slightly. Cook, stirring frequently, until the yam has
browned. Remove from the heat and serve.

Indian Cheese Balls

Sanar Kofta

The Indian cheese known as paneer in the rest of the country is called sana in north-east India and Bengal. In this recipe, grated paneer is mixed with mashed potatoes and a few chosen spices, formed into small balls and browned before being simmered in a spicy sauce. Paneer provides as much protein as meat, fish and poultry and is a very popular ingredient among India's vegetarian population. The cheese, which is regularly made in Indian households, can be used instantly as it requires no maturing time. Paneer is often referred to as 'Indian cottage cheese' and can be cooked in a variety of ways in both sweet and savoury dishes.

1 Put the cheese, potatoes, 5ml/1 tsp of the ginger purée, chopped green chilli, garam masala, egg, coriander leaves and half the salt in a bowl and mix thoroughly. Make about 16 equal-sized balls out of the mixture.

2 In a non-stick pan, heat 30ml/2 tbsp of the oil over a medium heat and brown the cheese balls evenly. Drain on kitchen paper.

3 Add the remaining oil to the pan and stir in the cardamom and cinnamon. Let them sizzle for a few seconds, then add the onion and fry until it is beginning to brown. Add the remaining ginger purée and the garlic and cook for about a minute. Add the turmeric, chilli powder, coriander and cumin and stir-fry for another minute or so, then pour in 300ml/10fl oz/1¼ cups warm water and add the remaining salt. Bring the mixture to the boil and cook over a medium heat for 2–3 minutes.

4 Add the browned cheese balls in a single layer and spoon over some of the sauce. Add the peas and whole chillies, reduce the heat to low, and cook for 5–6 minutes or until the sauce has thickened to the desired consistency. Serve with plain boiled rice.

Serves 4

225g/8oz/2 cups paneer, grated

200g/7oz/1 cup cooked potatoes, mashed

10ml/2 tsp ginger purée

1 green chilli, chopped (seeded if you like)

2.5ml/½ tsp garam masala

1 egg, beaten

30ml/2 tbsp coriander (cilantro) leaves, finely chopped

2.5ml/½ tsp salt or to taste

60ml/4 tbsp sunflower oil or plain olive oil

4 green cardamom pods, bruised

2.5cm/1in piece of cinnamon stick

1 large onion, finely chopped

5ml/1 tsp garlic purée

2.5ml/½ tsp ground turmeric

2.5–5ml/½–1 tsp chilli powder

5ml/1 tsp ground coriander

5ml/1 tsp ground cumin

150g/5oz frozen garden peas

3–4 whole green chillies

PER PORTION Energy 263kcal/1097kJ; Protein 12.2g; Carbohydrate 20.4g, of which sugars 8.8g; Fat 15.5g, of which saturates 3g; Cholesterol 55mg; Calcium 89mg; Fibre 2.3g; Sodium 242mg.

Duck Eggs with Cauliflower

Hahor Koni aru Phoolkobi

Duck eggs are very popular in the north-east, but hen's eggs are also perfectly suitable for this recipe. This dish was created by my mother who was a superb cook. Lightly spiced and crunchy cauliflower florets are embraced by golden eggs accentuated with fresh chillies and coriander leaves. The cauliflower is highly nutritious because it contains selenium and vitamin C, both of which are beneficial to the immune system. It is also rich in fibre and energy-boosting folate. This dish is a perfect protein-rich vegetarian main meal that goes particularly well with spicy lentils or any kind of rice – especially pilau rice. It also tastes really good when wrapped in Wholemeal Flat Bread or served with Deep-fried Puffed Bread.

Serves 4

- 1 medium-sized cauliflower (450g/1lb approx), divided into 2.5cm/1in florets
- 45ml/3 tbsp sunflower oil or plain olive oil
- 2.5ml/½ tsp black mustard seeds
- 5ml/1 tsp cumin seeds, lightly crushed
- 5ml/1 tsp coriander seeds, lightly crushed
- 2.5ml/½ tsp nigella seeds
- 1 medium onion, finely sliced
- 1–2 green chillies, finely chopped (seeded if you like)
- 5ml/1 tsp ground turmeric
- 2.5ml/½ tsp salt or to taste
- 30ml/2 tbsp coriander (cilantro) leaves, finely chopped
- 4 duck eggs, beaten

1 Blanch the cauliflower florets in boiling salted water for 3 minutes, drain and immediately plunge in iced water to stop them cooking further.

2 Heat the oil in a non-stick wok or a frying pan over a medium heat. When hot, but not smoking, throw in the mustard seeds, and as soon as they pop, add the cumin, coriander and nigella seeds. Let the seeds crackle for a few seconds, then add the onion and chillies and stir-fry until the onion is soft, but not brown. Add the turmeric.

3 Drain the cauliflower and add to the pan along with the salt. Stir until the cauliflower is heated through, then add the coriander leaves. Pour the beaten eggs on top evenly and let them set for about 2 minutes. Stir the pan until the eggs coat the cauliflower and remove from the heat. Serve with Wholemeal Flat Breads and/or plain boiled rice and Red Split Lentils with Mustard and Cumin.

PER PORTION Energy 264kcal/1095kJ; Protein 16.1g; Carbohydrate 7.9g, of which sugars 4.5g; Fat 19g, of which saturates 3.5g; Cholesterol 509mg; Calcium 90mg; Fibre 2.5g; Sodium 103mg.

Garlic-flavoured Mung Beans with Courgettes

Khar

Khar is made in a variety of ways in Assam and is always served at the beginning of a meal, as it is believed to aid digestion. However it is not really an appetizer, but part of the main meal. Bicarbonate of soda is used here to replace the traditional ingredient of burnt ashes of the banana tree trunk, known as kharoni. The nutritional value of mung beans cannot be stressed highly enough. They have no saturated fat, are rich in dietary fibre, protein, iron, vitamin C and plenty of other nutrients. Once soaked, they can be eaten raw in salads or stir-fried with garlic, chillies and sweet red peppers. Mung beans can be served hot or cold.

1 Wash the mung beans and soak them for 6–8 hours or overnight.

2 Heat 45ml/3 tbsp of the mustard oil over a medium heat until it reaches smoking point. Switch off the heat and add the fenugreek. When the seeds go a shade darker, add the garlic, half the ginger and the chillies. Put the heat back on to medium and stir-fry the ingredients for 1–2 minutes.

3 Drain the soaked mung beans and add to the pan. Stir-fry for 3–4 minutes and add the bicarbonate of soda and salt. Next, pour in 600ml/1 pint/2½ cups warm water and bring the mixture to the boil. Reduce the heat slightly and cook for 12–15 minutes or until the beans are tender.

4 Add the diced courgette and cook for a further 4–5 minutes. Remove from the heat and stir in the reserved mustard oil and ginger. Serve with plain boiled rice.

Serves 4

225g/8oz/1¼ cups mung beans

60ml/4 tbsp mustard oil

8–10 fenugreek seeds

4–5 large garlic cloves, crushed

8cm/3in piece of fresh root ginger, grated

1 fresh red chilli, sliced diagonally (seeded if you like)

1 fresh green chilli, sliced diagonally (seeded if you like)

2.5ml/½ tsp bicarbonate of soda (baking soda)

5ml/1 tsp salt or to taste

1 courgette (zucchini), finely diced

PER PORTION Energy 268kcal/1125kJ; Protein 13.5g; Carbohydrate 27g, of which sugars 1.5g; Fat 12.6g, of which saturates 1.6g; Cholesterol 0mg; Calcium 70mg; Fibre 8.8g; Sodium 13mg.

Red Split Lentils with Mustard and Cumin
Daail

In a country where the vast majority of the population is vegetarian, lentils provide all the nutrients required for a healthy diet, and regularly form part of a family meal. 'Dhal', 'dal' or 'daail' are cooked in different corners of the country with their own distinctive combination of spices to produce an utterly satisfying and perfectly healthy diet. Red split lentils and skinless split mung beans are frequently cooked in an Assamese kitchen, with the tarka (seasoning) based on mustard oil. For a richer flavour, this recipe uses a mixture of ghee and sunflower oil. This protein- and fibre-rich dish not only provides sustenance and nourishment, but is also an inexpensive meal.

1 Wash the lentils and mung beans thoroughly and drain. Put them in a pan with the turmeric and add 1 litre/1¾ pints/4 cups water.

2 Bring to the boil and remove any froth with a slotted spoon. Let them boil for 3–5 minutes, reduce the heat to low and cover the pan. Simmer for 30–35 minutes, then stir in the salt. Stir the lentils once or twice during cooking.

3 Heat the ghee or butter and oil in a small pan over a medium heat until almost smoking. Turn the heat off and throw in the mustard and cumin seeds, followed by the chillies and bay leaves. Allow the chillies to blacken slightly, then turn the heat back on to medium.

4 Add the onion and stir-fry until the onion turns golden brown. Add all the cooked spices to the lentils and mix well.

5 Stir in the coriander leaves and remove from the heat. Serve with Wholemeal Flat Bread and/or plain boiled rice.

Serves 4

115g/4oz/½ cup red split lentils
115g/4oz/½ cup skinless split mung beans (mung dhal)
2.5ml/½ tsp ground turmeric
5ml/1 tsp salt or to taste
25g/1oz/2 tbsp ghee or unsalted butter
30ml/2 tbsp sunflower oil
2.5ml/½ tsp mustard seeds
2.5ml/½ tsp cumin seeds
2 dried red chillies, whole
2 bay leaves
1 small onion, finely chopped
30ml/2 tbsp coriander (cilantro) leaves, finely chopped

To garnish:
Julienne strips of fresh tomato

PER PORTION Energy 263kcal/1110kJ; Protein 15.2g; Carbohydrate 36.6g, of which sugars 2.2g; Fat 7.1g, of which saturates 1g; Cholesterol 0mg; Calcium 49mg; Fibre 3g; Sodium 24mg.

Serves 4

700g/1½ lb potatoes

4 hard-boiled eggs

5ml/1 tsp salt or to taste

30ml/2 tbsp mustard oil

2 shallots, finely chopped

1 green chilli, finely chopped (seeded if you like)

30ml/2 tbsp coriander (cilantro) leaves, finely chopped

To garnish:
Julienne strips of fresh red chillies

PER PORTION Energy 150kcal/622kJ; Protein 7.2g; Carbohydrate 5.9g, of which sugars 4.2g; Fat 11.2g, of which saturates 2.1g; Cholesterol 190mg; Calcium 47mg; Fibre 1.1g; Sodium 72mg.

Crushed Potatoes with Chopped Hard-boiled Eggs

Alu-Konir Pitika

This classic dish can be enjoyed any time of day. Boiled potatoes are crushed and combined with chopped hard-boiled eggs and flavoured with mustard oil, finely chopped shallots, green chilli and fresh coriander leaves. It is one of those comforting dishes that you can snack on at any time.

1 Peel and boil the potatoes until they are soft, then mash them. Chop the egg whites and mash the yolks. Combine the eggs and potatoes and add all the remaining ingredients. Mix well.

2 Set the mixture in 4 ring moulds or small bowls and garnish with the red chilli strips. Serve with Garlic-flavoured Mung Beans with Courgettes and plain boiled rice for a typical Assamese meal.

Egg Fritters

Konir Bora

These are great at buffet or drinks parties as well as making a delicious first course with a salad garnish. Hard-boiled eggs are chopped and mixed with breadcrumbs and spices, then fried until crisp – just the sort of snack to eat sitting in front of the fire on a cold, wintry evening.

1 Put the bread in a food processor and process it into crumbs. Add the coriander, chillies, ginger, fennel, salt and beaten egg. Process until the mixture is well blended, then add the hard-boiled eggs and chop them roughly using the pulse action.

2 Transfer the mixture into a bowl and make 12 equal-sized portions. Form each portion into a ball and flatten to a smooth round cake.

3 Heat the oil in a wok or other suitable pan over medium/high heat. Dust each cake in the cornflour, shaking off any excess.

4 Fry the cakes in batches until crisp and golden brown and then drain on kitchen paper. Arrange the fritters on a bed of the garnish ingredients listed and serve with a chutney of your choice.

Makes 12

2 slices white bread, a day or two old, crusts removed

30–45ml/2–3 tbsp coriander (cilantro) leaves and stalks

1–2 green chillies, chopped (seeded if you like)

1cm/½in piece of root ginger, peeled and chopped

5ml/1 tsp fennel seeds

2.5ml/½ tsp salt

1 medium egg, beaten

4 large hard-boiled eggs

15ml/1 tbsp cornflour (cornstarch)

Oil for deep frying

To garnish:

Mixed lettuce leaves, red onion rings, diced cucumber

PER PORTION Energy 307kcal/1278kJ; Protein 25.1g; Carbohydrate 3.8g, of which sugars 0.1g; Fat 22g, of which saturates 6.1g; Cholesterol 745mg; Calcium 119mg; Fibre 0.1g; Sodium 299mg.

Plain Boiled Rice

Boga Bhaat

Many people worry about how to cook rice successfully. For the best and healthiest method follow the steps described below. You should alway wash the rice first, which removes most of the milling starch, then soak it for 20 minutes before cooking, and, last but not least, once the lid goes on the pan, simply time it and do not lift the lid until the cooking time is over.

1 Wash the rice thoroughly until the water runs clear, then soak it in cold water for 20 minutes and drain.

2 Put the rice in a heavy pan and add the butter and salt. Pour in 450ml/16fl oz/2 cups hot water. Bring it to the boil and let it cook, uncovered, for 2–3 minutes.

3 Reduce the heat to very low, cover the pan with a tight-fitting lid and cook for 7–8 minutes. Remove from the heat and allow it to stand undisturbed for 7–8 minutes. Fluff up the rice with a fork and transfer to a serving dish. Serve with just about any curry.

Serves 4

225g/8oz/1¼ cups basmati rice
5ml/1 tsp butter
2.5ml/½ tsp salt or to taste

PER PORTION Energy 211kcal/883kJ; Protein 4.2g; Carbohydrate 44.9g, of which sugars 0g; Fat 1.3g, of which saturates 0.7g; Cholesterol 3mg; Calcium 11mg; Fibre 0g; Sodium 10mg.

Makes 8

400g/14oz/3½ cups chapati flour (atta) or
  fine wholemeal (whole-wheat) flour
5ml/1 tsp salt
30ml/2 tbsp sunflower oil or plain olive oil
250ml/8fl oz/1 cup lukewarm water
A little extra flour for dusting
Sunflower oil or plain olive oil for frying

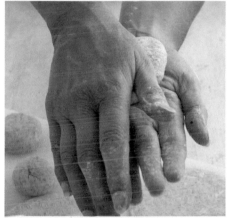

PER PORTION Energy 180kcal/761kJ; Protein 6.4g;
Carbohydrate 32g, of which sugars 1.1g; Fat 3.9g, of which
saturates 0.5g; Cholesterol 0mg; Calcium 19mg; Fibre 4.5g;
Sodium 247mg.

Wholemeal Flat Bread

Ruti

These breads are thicker than chapatis and are griddle-cooked, with oil or ghee spread over the surface. Unlike the dough for chapatis and phulkas, this mixture contains a small amount of fat and warm water is used instead of cold.

1 Mix the flour and salt together in a mixing bowl. Add the oil and work well into the flour with your fingertips. Gradually add the water, continuing to mix until a dough is formed. Transfer it to a flat surface and knead it for 4–5 minutes. When all the excess moisture is absorbed by the flour, wrap the dough in clear film (plastic wrap) and let it rest for 30 minutes. Alternatively, make the dough in a food processor.

2 Divide the dough into 8 even balls and make flat cakes by rotating them between the palms and pressing them down. Roll out each cake on a floured surface into a 13cm/5in circle.

3 Pre-heat a heavy cast-iron or other similar griddle over a medium heat and place a rolled disc on it. Allow to cook for 2 minutes, then turn it over. Spread 5ml/1 tsp oil evenly on the surface and turn it over again. Cook for 2 minutes until browned all over. Spread 5ml/1 tsp oil on the second side, turn the bread over, and cook as above until browned. Keep the cooked breads hot by wrapping them in a piece of foil lined with kitchen paper or a clean dish towel. Cook the remaining flat breads in the same way. Serve with any curry.

Deep-fried Soft Puffed Bread

Kumol Lusi

These are similar to east India's luchi, but they are softer and richer. They are made with plain flour and the dough is enriched with ghee and hot milk, instead of water, creating a velvety soft bread. They are perfect with any vegetable curry and are also popular with spiced omelettes and Indian-style scrambled eggs. A healthier version can be made by using wholemeal flour and adding olive oil instead of ghee. This creates a wholesome taste that complements most vegetable curries, lentils, beans and peas.

1 Sift the flour into a large bowl and add the salt, sugar and ghee or butter. Mix the ingredients well and gradually add the milk. Mix until a soft dough is formed, then transfer it to a flat surface. Knead for 4–5 minutes. Alternatively, make the dough in a food processor. Wrap the dough in clear film (plastic wrap) and let it rest for 20–30 minutes.

2 Divide the dough into 2 equal parts and make 8 equal-sized balls out of each. Flatten the balls into cakes by rotating and pressing them between your palms.

3 Dust each cake very lightly in the flour and roll them out to about 6cm/2½in circles, taking care not to tear or pierce them, as they will not puff up if damaged. Place them in a single layer on a piece of baking parchment and cover with another piece.

4 Heat the oil in a wok or other suitable pan for deep-frying, over a medium/high heat. When the oil has a faint shimmer of rising smoke on the surface, carefully drop in one dough cake and as soon as it floats, gently tap round the edges to encourage puffing. When it has puffed up, turn it over and fry the other side until browned.

5 Drain on kitchen paper. Keep the fried breads on a tray in a single layer. They are best eaten fresh, although they can be reheated briefly (3–4 minutes) in a moderately hot oven. Serve with Egg, Potato and Green Pea Curry or Duck Eggs with Cauliflower.

Makes 16

275g/10oz/2½ cups plain (all-purpose) flour, plus a little extra for dusting
2.5ml/½ tsp salt
1.5ml/¼ tsp sugar
15ml/1 tbsp ghee or unsalted (sweet) butter
175ml/6fl oz/⅔ cup lukewarm milk
Oil for deep frying

PER PORTION Energy 72kcal/306kJ; Protein 2g; Carbohydrate 14g, of which sugars 0.9g; Fat 1.3g, of which saturates 0.6g; Cholesterol 1mg; Calcium 37mg; Fibre 0.5g; Sodium 68mg.

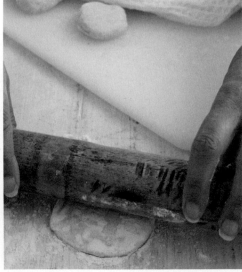

Serves 4–5

350ml/12fl oz/1½ cups canned
  coconut milk

110g/4oz/½ cup palm sugar (jaggery),
  grated, or dark brown sugar

225g/8oz/2 cups plain (all-purpose) flour

Pinch bicarbonate of soda (baking soda)

5ml/1 tsp ground cardamom

1.5ml/¼ tsp ground nutmeg

5ml/1 tsp nigella seeds

25g/1oz seedless raisins

Oil for deep frying

150ml/5fl oz/⅔ cup single (light) cream

To decorate:

A few pomegranate seeds or other
  seasonal fruit

PER PORTION Energy 393kcal/1657kJ; Protein 6.9g;
Carbohydrate 66.3g, of which sugars 31.9g; Fat 12.9g, of
which saturates 2.1g; Cholesterol 4mg; Calcium 161mg;
Fibre 1.6g; Sodium 55mg.

Cardamom-scented Coconut Dumplings
Narikolor Malpuwa

Sweet coconut dumplings with the heady aroma of crushed cardamom are a teatime treat. They are also served for breakfast in Assam, as a dessert with fresh fruits and cream, or even as wonderful sweet snacks at buffet parties.

1 Put the coconut milk into a small pan and add the grated palm sugar or dark brown sugar. Place over a low heat and stir until the sugar is completely dissolved. Leave to cool.

2 Sift the flour into a mixing bowl and add the bicarbonate of soda, cardamom, nutmeg, nigella seeds and raisins. Mix well. Add the cooled, sweetened coconut milk and mix until a thick batter is formed.

3 Heat the oil in a wok or other pan suitable for deep-frying over a low/medium heat. Using a dessert spoon, put in as many spoonfuls of the batter as the pan will hold comfortably in a single layer. Do not overcrowd the pan. Fry them gently for 7–8 minutes, reducing the heat if necessary, until the dumplings are well browned. Drain on kitchen paper.

4 Pour the cream into a pan and heat gently until just simmering. Add the dumplings and stir them around until they are well coated, and the cream has thickened slightly. Remove from the heat and cool. Serve garnished with the pomegranate seeds. These dumplings can also be served on their own without any cream or fruit.

Black Sesame Seed Fudge

Tilor Borfi

Sesame seeds grow widely throughout India. They come in all shades from pale ivory to brown and black. The ivory seeds are used to enrich and thicken curries, while the black ones are used mainly in the north-east regions to make delicious sweetmeats. If black seeds prove difficult to find, ivory ones can be used in this recipe.

1 Dry-roast the sesame seeds and the cardamom pods in a heavy pan over a medium heat, stirring constantly for 7–8 minutes. Transfer them to a large plate and let them cool. When cold, grind them in a food processor.

2 Put the sugar in a heavy pan and add 200ml/7fl oz/¾ cup water. Place over a medium heat and bring to the boil. Cook for about 2 minutes and then add the ground sesame seeds. Stir over a medium heat until the mixture stops sticking to the bottom and sides of the pan (5–6 minutes).

3 Brush a 30cm/12in plate with a little oil and spread the sesame mixture on it. Push the sides in with the back of a metal spoon to make a complete square about 1cm/½in thick.

4 Rub the peanuts with a clean cloth to remove some of the salt and split them into halves. Press them gently on to the surface of the sesame fudge, leave to cool and chill for an hour or two before cutting into squares or diamonds. Serve with afternoon tea or after-dinner coffee.

Serves 6

350g/12oz/generous 2 cups black
  sesame seeds

5 green cardamom pods, bruised

150g/5oz/⅔ cup palm sugar (jaggery),
  grated, or dark brown soft sugar

200ml/7fl oz/¾ cup water

25g/1oz roasted peanuts

PER PORTION Energy 471kcal/1959kJ; Protein 11.8g; Carbohydrate 27.2g, of which sugars 26.6g; Fat 35.8g, of which saturates 5.2g; Cholesterol 0mg; Calcium 407mg; Fibre 4.9g; Sodium 13mg.

east india

The cuisine of east India is associated with the British Raj, and the local Bengali cooking is highly popular throughout the country. Fish curry features heavily in the Bengali daily diet, but a variety of vegetarian dishes cooked in nutty mustard oil with a liberal use of the famous Bengali creation, the aromatic panchphoron, are eaten every day. Delicous recipes from this region include Spiced Potato Cakes, Cinnamon and Clove-scented Cheese Curry, Lemon-laced Rice with Cardamom, and Vegetable Pilau.

Flavours of east India

The three east-Indian states, west Bengal, Bihar and Orissa, provide some of the most stunning contrasts in the landscape of this region. Lush Gangetic plains, magnificent mountains and rolling tea plantations, together with huge lakes and rivers, make a breathtaking sight. The most famous city in east India is Kolkata (formerly Calcutta), which is 300 years old and is the capital of west Bengal.

Bengali cuisine is typified by pungent mustard oil made from locally grown mustard. Root ginger, turmeric and pepper crops thrive, and rice, the staple diet, is cultivated throughout the region. Bengalis love fish, but there is also a huge repertoire of vegetarian food with complex flavours and intensely aromatic tastes. They cook these in mustard oil and flavour them with aromatic panchphoron and locally grown turmeric. The Bengali tradition that widows follow a strict vegetarian diet has helped create some unusual recipes using vegetables such as banana blossom, bottle gourd, ridge gourd and drumsticks (a long, stringy green vegetable).

Dairy products are also an important part of the Bengali diet, especially since they provide plenty of protein to the vegetarian population. A magnificent spectrum of desserts and sweetmeats are dairy-based, and Bengal's contribution to the national cuisine is incomparable in this field. Prime examples are gulab jamoon, which are fried milk puffs in sugar syrup, sandesh, which is a kind of soft fudge made from fresh cheese, and cinnamon-scented rice pudding. These sweet treats are all highly popular throughout the country.

Darjeeling, located in close proximity to some of the highest peaks of the Himalayas, is surrounded by rolling tea plantations. Darjeeling tea is renowned the world over for its delicate bouquet and an inimitable taste.

The state of Bihar has striking geographical features with thick woods and a succession of hilly and flat terrain. The climate is quite extreme in both summer and winter. The main crops are rice, wheat, maize, beans, peas and lentils. The people of Bihar belong to the Hindu and Buddhist faiths, both of which are based on the principles of 'Ahimsa', meaning non-violence. This forbids them to eat meat, fish, eggs and any animal product. The food here is, therefore, mainly vegetarian. As in Bengal, Biharis use panchphoron to flavour their vegetables and pulses, all of which are cooked in mustard oil. Bihari thali (platter) is generally made up of seasonal vegetables and a flat bread, and dairy products, such as yogurt, ghee (clarified butter) and lassi (a yogurt drink), are also very popular.

The state of Orissa is situated in the tropical zone and enjoys an equable climate. Orissa relies heavily on agriculture and rice, sugarcane, coconut and turmeric are the main crops produced in the region and the staple food of the locals is rice. Ingredients are cooked in coconut-based sauces and flavoured with the renowned Bengali seasoning panchphoron, called panch phutana in this area. Orissa excels in the use of the banana tree. The fruit and other various tree parts are imaginatively spiced and skilfully cooked. In summer, fermented rice with home-made yogurt or pakhala is eaten to help to lower the body temperature.

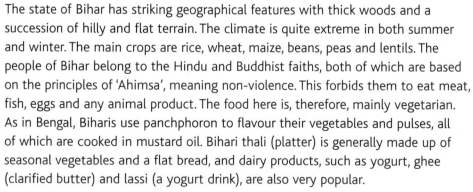

Spiced Potato Cakes
Alur Bora

This Bengali recipe for delicious deep-fried spiced potato cakes brings back fond memories of the many happy times I spent in the kitchen with my mother. We always enjoyed these potato cakes at afternoon tea, which is still a big occasion in this part of the country, a legacy left behind by the British tea plantation owners. These tasty potato cakes can easily be frozen and reheated in a hot oven for 10–12 minutes – perfect for those unexpected guests.

1 In a small pan, heat the oil over a medium heat and add the fennel seeds. Allow them to sizzle for a few seconds, then add the onion, chillies and ginger. Fry for 3–4 minutes until the onions become soft.

2 Stir in the turmeric, coriander leaves and salt, and remove from the heat.

3 Put the mashed potato in a mixing bowl and add the spice mixture, mix well and add the cornflour and egg. Stir until all the ingredients are well blended.

4 Heat the oil for deep-frying in a wok or other suitable pan over a medium/high heat. Drop a tiny amount of the potato mixture into the oil to test the temperature. If the potato mixture starts sizzling and floats to the top immediately, then the oil is at the right temperature.

5 Take 15ml/1 tbsp of the potato mixture, and with two spoons, make a rough croquette shape, then gently lower it into the hot oil. Fry as many potato cakes as the pan will hold in a single layer without overcrowding it. Fry until the cakes are well browned (5–6 minutes) and drain on kitchen paper. Serve with Roasted Tomato Chutney.

Serves 4–5

30ml/2 tbsp sunflower oil or vegetable oil

2.5ml/½ tsp fennel seeds

1 medium onion, finely chopped

1–2 green chillies, chopped (seeded if you like)

10ml/2 tsp ginger purée

2.5ml/½ tsp ground turmeric

30ml/2 tbsp coriander (cilantro) leaves, chopped

5ml/1 tsp salt or to taste

450g/1lb potatoes, boiled and lightly mashed

15ml/1 tbsp cornflour (cornstarch)

1 large egg, beaten

Oil for deep frying

Cook's Tip

It is important to avoid putting too many potato cakes together in the frying pan as it will lower the temperature of the oil and cause them to break up.

PER PORTION Energy 256kcal/1064kJ; Protein 3.8g; Carbohydrate 23.6g, of which sugars 5.7g; Fat 16.9g, of which saturates 2.3g; Cholesterol 38mg; Calcium 32mg; Fibre 2g; Sodium 421mg.

Spiced Aubergine with Hard-boiled Egg

Khagina

Khagina is similar to the north-Indian dish bharta, but the addition of chopped hard-boiled eggs makes all the difference in taste, texture and appearance. In days gone by, khagina graced many buffet tables of the British-influenced clubs in Kolkata (formerly Calcutta). Khagina still remains a favourite dish in most of these establishments as Kolkata still has strong evidence of British occupation. The aubergine can be cooked and frozen in advance then re-heated before adding the chopped eggs. Another lovely way of serving the smoked aubergine is to top it with small stir-fried spiced prawns.

1 Pre-heat the grill (broiler) to high and make at least two small incisions in the aubergine to prevent it from bursting during cooking. Rub a little oil all over the aubergine, place it approximately 15cm/6in below the heat source and grill (broil) for 8–10 minutes, turning it over halfway through. Remove and cool.

2 When the aubergine is cool enough to handle, slit it lengthways into two halves and scrape out the flesh with a knife or a spoon. Discard the skin and chop the flesh finely.

3 Heat the oil over a medium heat and add the mustard seeds; as soon as they start popping, add the fennel and nigella seeds. Allow all the seeds to sizzle gently for 15–20 seconds, then add the onion, ginger and chilli, and stir-fry until the onion is beginning to turn brown.

4 Add the turmeric and cumin and stir-fry for 30–40 seconds. Add the aubergine flesh and the chopped tomato and stir-fry for 1–2 minutes, then add the chopped eggs, coriander leaves and salt. Cook for about a minute and remove from the heat. Serve with strips of naan or on small savoury biscuits (crackers).

Serves 4

- 1 large aubergine (eggplant), approximately 350g/12oz
- 45ml/3 tbsp sunflower oil or plain olive oil
- 2.5ml/½ tsp mustard seeds
- 2.5ml/½ tsp fennel seeds
- 2.5ml/½ tsp nigella seeds
- 1 medium onion, finely chopped
- 5ml/1 tsp ginger purée
- 1 green chilli, chopped (seeded if you like)
- 2.5ml/½ tsp ground turmeric
- 2.5ml/½ tsp ground cumin
- 1 ripe tomato, skinned and chopped
- 2 hard-boiled eggs, roughly chopped
- 15g/1½oz fresh coriander (cilantro), including the tender stalks, roughly chopped
- 2.5ml/½ tsp salt

PER PORTION Energy 173kcal/719kJ; Protein 6g; Carbohydrate 10.6g, of which sugars 6.6g; Fat 12.4g, of which saturates 2g; Cholesterol 95mg; Calcium 62mg; Fibre 3.2g; Sodium 44mg.

Spiced Lentil-filled Pancakes
Pittha

From the little-known cuisine of the state of Bihar, this recipe for pancakes filled with spiced lentils is wholesome and healthy as well as tasting delicious. The pancakes are very versatile – they can be served as an appetizer, a hearty brunch, or as a teatime snack. They can also be frozen, then defrosted and shallow-fried when needed.

1 Wash the split chickpeas in several changes of water and soak for 4–5 hours or overnight.

2 Drain the split chickpeas and put into a food processor with the garlic, ginger and both types of chillies. Blend to a fine paste, adding 30–45ml/2–3 tbsp water if necessary.

3 Put the paste into a non-stick pan with the turmeric and asafoetida. Cook, stirring constantly, until the mixture is dry and crumbly. Remove from the heat and transfer it to a mixing bowl. Add the yogurt, coriander leaves and salt and mix thoroughly. If the mixture is still slightly crumbly, add a little water to make it into a paste-like consistency. Allow to cool.

4 Meanwhile, make the pastry. Mix both types of flour and the salt in a mixing bowl, then gradually add the water (the amount needed will depend on the absorbency of the flour). When the dough has formed, transfer it to a flat surface and knead it until soft and pliable.

5 Wrap the dough in clear film (plastic wrap) and allow it to rest for 30 minutes, then divide it into 12 portions and make each portion into a flat cake. Keep them covered with a damp cloth while you are working on one at a time. Roll out each cake into roughly a 10cm/4in circle.

6 Divide the filling into 12 equal parts and place a portion on one half of a circle. Moisten the edges and enclose the filling by folding over the other half, making a half-moon shape. Press to seal and crimp the edges with the back of a fork. Cook the pancakes in a steamer for 25 minutes. Serve with Roasted Tomato Chutney.

Makes 12

For the filling:
225g/8oz/1 cup skinless split chickpeas (channa dhal)
2 large garlic cloves, chopped
2.5cm/1in piece of fresh root ginger, peeled and chopped
2 dried red chillies, chopped
1 green chilli, chopped (seeded if you like)
2.5ml/½ tsp ground turmeric
2.5ml/½ tsp asafoetida
50g/2oz/¼ cup natural (plain) yogurt
30ml/2 tbsp coriander (cilantro) leaves, chopped
5ml/1 tsp salt or to taste

For the pastry:
150g/5oz/1¼ cups chapati flour (atta) or fine wholemeal (whole-wheat) flour
150g/5oz/1¼ cups plain (all-purpose) flour
2.5ml/½ tsp salt
200ml/7fl oz/¾ cup water
Extra flour for dusting

PER PORTION Energy 148kcal/630kJ; Protein 7.7g; Carbohydrate 29.2g, of which sugars 1.2g; Fat 0.9g, of which saturates 0.2g; Cholesterol 0mg; Calcium 43mg; Fibre 2.4g; Sodium 12mg.

Vegetable Pilau

Torkarir Pulao

The climate and soil conditions mean that rice flourishes in Bengal, and it has become the staple diet of the Bengali people. Plain boiled rice is served at every meal, with lentils, vegetables and fish. This colourful creation with basmati rice and fresh vegetables is ideal as a vegetarian main meal, accompanied by plain yogurt. The choice of vegetables can be varied according to seasonal availability and individual taste.

1 Wash the rice until the water runs clear and soak it for 20 minutes. Leave the rice to drain in a colander.

2 In a heavy pan, heat the oil over a medium/low heat and brown the cashew nuts. Drain on kitchen paper. Add the raisins and fry until they are puffed. Drain on kitchen paper. Briefly frying the raisins softens them, giving them a luscious texture and superb taste.

3 Add the cardamom, cinnamon, cloves and bay leaves to the remaining oil and let them sizzle until the cardamoms have puffed up. Add the onion, ginger, garlic and chillies, increase the heat slightly and fry until the onion is golden brown, stirring regularly.

4 Stir in the turmeric and add all the vegetables and the salt. Stir and cook for 2–3 minutes, then add the rice. Stir-fry for 2–3 minutes. Pour in 450ml/16fl oz/1¾ cups hot water and bring it to the boil. Allow to boil steadily for 2 minutes, then reduce the heat to low.

5 Sprinkle the cream evenly over the rice and cover the pan tightly. Cook for 10–12 minutes. Remove from the heat and leave the pan undisturbed, without lifting the lid, for 8–10 minutes. Fluff up the rice and serve, garnished with the nuts and raisins. A plain yogurt raita is all you will need to accompany this pilau.

Serves 4

225g/8oz/generous 1 cup basmati rice

60ml/4 tbsp sunflower oil or plain olive oil

25g/1oz raw cashew nuts

25g/1oz seedless raisins

4 green cardamom pods, bruised

2.5cm/1in piece of cinnamon stick

4 cloves

2 bay leaves

1 large onion, finely sliced

5ml/1 tsp ginger purée

5ml/1 tsp garlic purée

1–2 green chillies, chopped (seeded if you like)

2.5ml/½ tsp ground turmeric

75g/3oz/½ cup carrots, cut into sticks

110g/4oz baby corn, halved

75g/3oz/½ cup green beans, cut into 2.5cm/1in lengths

5ml/1 tsp salt or to taste

50ml/2fl oz/3 tbsp single (light) cream

PER PORTION Energy 410kcal/1705kJ; Protein 8.1g; Carbohydrate 60.9g, of which sugars 12.5g; Fat 14.9g, of which saturates 2g; Cholesterol 0mg; Calcium 55mg; Fibre 3g; Sodium 343mg.

Cinnamon and Clove-scented Cheese Curry
Channer Dalna

Indian cheese (paneer) is a great source of protein and the vast majority of the Indian population thrive on this versatile ingredient, which is used for both savoury and sweet dishes. Paneer is available in large supermarkets and Indian stores. It is often made in Indian households as it requires no maturing time. It has a bland taste, but readily absorbs other flavours, and when cooked in a sauce it develops a melt-in-the-mouth, tender texture.

1 Heat half the oil in a non-stick pan over a medium heat and brown the cubes of paneer. Stand well away from the pan while frying the paneer as it tends to splutter. Drain the cubes on kitchen paper. Dry the cubes of potato with a cloth and brown them in the same oil. Drain on kitchen paper.

2 Add the remaining oil to the pan and reduce the heat to low. Add the cinnamon, cardamom and cloves; let them sizzle until the cardamom pods have puffed up. Add the onion and increase the heat slightly. Cook for 5–6 minutes until the onion has softened, then add the ginger and garlic and fry until the onion is beginning to brown. Add the turmeric, chilli powder and cumin and cook for about a minute. Next, add 30ml/2 tbsp water, and cook until the mixture is dry and the water has evaporated. Repeat this process twice more (adding 90ml/6 tbsp water in all).

3 Add the browned potatoes, salt and 250ml/8fl oz/1 cup warm water to the pan. Bring the mixture to the boil, reduce the heat to low, cover the pan and simmer for 10 minutes. Add the browned paneer, increase the heat to medium and cook uncovered for 5–6 minutes or until the sauce has thickened.

4 Add the garam masala and coriander leaves, stir well and remove from the heat. Serve with any Indian bread.

Serves 4

60ml/4 tbsp sunflower oil or plain olive oil
225g/8oz/2 cups paneer, cut into 2.5cm/1in cubes
400g/14oz potatoes, cut into 2.5cm/1in cubes
2.5cm/1in piece of cinnamon stick
4 green cardamom pods, bruised
4 cloves
1 large onion, finely chopped
5ml/1 tsp ginger purée
5ml/1 tsp garlic purée
2.5ml/½ tsp ground turmeric
2.5–5ml/½–1 tsp chilli powder
2.5ml/½ tsp ground cumin
5ml/1 tsp salt or to taste
2.5ml/½ tsp garam masala
15ml/1 tbsp coriander (cilantro) leaves, chopped

PER PORTION Energy 280kcal/1170kJ; Protein 11.5g; Carbohydrate 28.5g, of which sugars 9.5g; Fat 14.2g, of which saturates 2.9g; Cholesterol 7mg; Calcium 85mg; Fibre 2.8g; Sodium 230mg.

Egg, Potato and Green Pea Curry

Dimer Dalna

In this classic dish, hard-boiled eggs and cubed boiled potatoes are flavoured with turmeric and chilli powder and shallow-fried to a rich golden colour before being simmered in an aromatic sauce. The jade-green peas, golden eggs and potato cubes doused in a rich-red sauce create a strikingly beautiful dish. Luchi is the traditional accompaniment to this delicious curry.

1 Shell the eggs and make four small slits in each without cutting them right through. Wash the potatoes and dry them with a cloth.

2 Heat the oil over a low heat and add 1.5ml/¼ tsp each of the turmeric and chilli powder, followed by the whole eggs. Stir the eggs around until they are coloured by the spices and develop a light golden crust. Remove the eggs and set them aside.

3 Add the potatoes to the same oil and increase the heat to medium. Stir-fry them until they are well browned and develop a light golden crust. Remove them with a slotted spoon and drain on kitchen paper.

4 Reduce the heat to low and add the cinnamon, cardamom, cloves and bay leaves and fry them for a few seconds. Add the onion, increase the heat to medium, and fry until the onion is golden brown (9–10 minutes).

5 On a low heat, add the ground coriander and cumin and the remaining turmeric and chilli powder. Stir-fry for 1 minute, then add the tomato and continue to cook for 1–2 minutes.

6 Add the browned potatoes, salt and sugar, and pour in 250ml/8fl oz/1 cup warm water. Bring the mixture to the boil, cover the pan and reduce the heat to low. Cook until the potatoes are al dente. Add the peas, cover the pan and cook for 5–6 minutes longer, until the potatoes are tender and the peas are cooked. Stir in the garam masala and remove from the heat. Serve with your favourite Indian bread.

Serves 4

4 hard-boiled eggs
350g/12oz medium-sized potatoes, peeled and quartered
60ml/4 tbsp sunflower oil or plain olive oil
2.5ml/½ tsp ground turmeric
2.5ml/½ tsp chilli powder
2.5cm/1in piece of cinnamon stick
4 green cardamom pods, bruised
4 cloves
2 bay leaves
1 large onion, finely chopped
5ml/1 tsp ground coriander
2.5ml/½ tsp ground cumin
1 fresh tomato, skinned and chopped
5ml/1 tsp salt or to taste
2.5ml/½ tsp sugar
115g/4oz/1 cup frozen peas, thawed, or pre-cooked fresh peas
2.5ml/½ tsp garam masala

PER PORTION Energy 316kcal/1317kJ; Protein 11.9g; Carbohydrate 29g, of which sugars 9.3g; Fat 18g, of which saturates 3.1g; Cholesterol 190mg; Calcium 79mg; Fibre 4.2g; Sodium 87mg.

Potatoes with Coriander and Sun-dried Mango

Aloo Chokha

In this recipe, cubed potatoes are adorned with crushed coriander seeds, red and green chillies and fresh coriander leaves. Sun-dried mango powder, known as amchur, is commonly used in Indian recipes and is sold in Asian shops. Sun-dried mango powder has an unmistakably distinctive sour taste, but if it proves difficult to find, lime juice can be used instead.

1 Heat the oil over a medium heat and add the onion with the green and red chillies. Fry, stirring regularly, until the onion is beginning to brown. Add the crushed coriander and stir-fry for about a minute. Add the cumin and turmeric, stir-fry for about a minute, then add the potatoes and salt. Pour in 250ml/8fl oz/1 cup warm water and bring it to the boil. Reduce the heat to low, cover the pan and cook for 12–15 minutes until the potatoes are tender and all the water has been absorbed.

2 Stir in the mango powder or lime juice and coriander leaves, and remove from the heat. Serve with a lentil dish and/or a vegetable curry, accompanied by Indian bread.

Serves 4

60ml/4 tbsp sunflower oil or plain olive oil

1 large onion, finely sliced

1–2 green chillies, chopped (seeded if you like)

1–2 dried red chillies, each sliced into 2–3 pieces

10ml/2 tsp coriander seeds, crushed

5ml/1 tsp ground cumin

2.5ml/½ tsp ground turmeric

450g/1lb potatoes, cut into 2.5cm/1in cubes

5ml/1 tsp salt or to taste

5ml/1 tsp sun-dried mango powder (amchur) or 15ml/1 tbsp lime juice

30ml/2 tbsp coriander (cilantro) leaves, chopped

PER PORTION Energy 237kcal/990kJ; Protein 4.2g; Carbohydrate 29.7g, of which sugars 8.5g; Fat 12.2g, of which saturates 1.5g; Cholesterol 0mg; Calcium 47mg; Fibre 2.9g; Sodium 509mg.

Makes 225g/8oz

700g/1½lb ripe tomatoes, halved

30ml/2 tbsp sunflower oil or plain olive oil

1–2 green chillies, chopped (seeded if
 you like)

1cm/½in piece of fresh root ginger,
 peeled and chopped

1 clove garlic, chopped

30ml/2 tbsp coriander (cilantro) leaves,
 chopped

2.5ml/½ tsp salt or to taste

Cook's Tip

The tomatoes can be cooked on a barbecue
for that traditional smoky flavour.

PER PORTION Energy 334kcal/1395kJ; Protein 6.4g;
Carbohydrate 23.1g, of which sugars 22.8g; Fat 24.7g, of
which saturates 3.3g; Cholesterol 0mg; Calcium 149mg;
Fibre 9.5g; Sodium 80mg.

Roasted Tomato Chutney

Tomato Achar

This delicious chutney recipe comes from Darjeeling, with definite
influences from Nepal, across the northern border. The Nepalese
would roast the tomatoes over a wood fire, which imparts an
unforgettable flavour. The tomatoes are then combined with chillies
and spices and made into a purée. A final seasoning is added with
sliced garlic and fenugreek seed. This chutney is best eaten fresh,
although it will keep in the refrigerator for up to one week.

1 Preheat the oven to 190°C/375°F/Gas 5.

2 Put the tomato halves in a roasting pan and drizzle the oil over them. Roast in the centre
of the oven for 20 minutes. Remove the tomatoes from the oven, leave them to cool and
then peel off the skin.

3 Place the roasted tomatoes in a blender or food processor along with all the remaining
ingredients and purée until smooth. Store in a sterilized, airtight jar and keep in the
refrigerator. Serve with all kinds of fried, grilled (broiled) and roasted appetizers or use
as a dip with poppadums.

Serves 4

225g/8oz/generous 1 cup basmati rice

50g/2oz/4 tbsp ghee or unsalted butter

25g/1oz raw cashew nuts

15ml/1 tbsp seedless raisins

1 large onion, finely sliced

2.5cm/1in piece of cinnamon stick

4 cloves

2 bay leaves

5ml/1 tsp salt or to taste

PER PORTION Energy 369kcal/1537kJ; Protein 5.8g; Carbohydrate 57.4g, of which sugars 9.6g; Fat 13g, of which saturates 5.9g; Cholesterol 0mg; Calcium 44mg; Fibre 1.8g; Sodium 6mg.

Butter-flavoured Rice with Spiced Stock

Ghee Bhat

Rice is eaten throughout India, but is most popular in areas where heavy rainfall results in thriving rice crops. This wonderful dish is cooked in ghee along with a few aromatic spices. The flavour of this rice is rich, but mild enough to go with any curry.

1 Wash the rice thoroughly and soak for 20 minutes. Leave to drain in a colander.

2 Melt half the ghee or butter over a low heat, then brown the cashew nuts. Drain the nuts on kitchen paper and set aside. Next, add the raisins and stir until they are plump. Drain these on kitchen paper and set aside.

3 Add the remaining ghee or butter to the pan and add the onion. Increase the heat to medium and fry the onion slices, stirring regularly, until they are well browned. Remove any excess fat by pressing the fried onions to the side of the pan, and then lift them out and drain them on kitchen paper.

4 Reduce the heat to low and add the cinnamon, cloves and bay leaves. Let them sizzle for 10–15 seconds, then add the drained rice and cook for 2 minutes. Pour in 450ml/16fl oz/ scant 2 cups hot water, add the salt, bring to the boil and cook for 2 minutes. Reduce the heat to very low, cover the pan and cook for 7–8 minutes without lifting the lid. Switch off the heat and leave the pan undisturbed for a further 7–8 minutes.

5 Fluff up the rice with a fork and gently mix in half the fried onions. Reserve a few cashews and raisins and mix the remainder into the rice. Transfer the rice to a serving dish and garnish with the remaining onion, cashews and raisins.

Lemon-laced Rice with Cardamom

Lebur Bhat

Bengali lemon-laced rice is rather different to the version that is cooked in south India. It has a more prominent lemon flavour, which smells and tastes wonderfully refreshing. Bay leaves, cardamom, cinnamon and cloves are commonly used in east India to flavour rice dishes. Mustard oil is also traditional, but you can replace it with sunflower or olive oil if you prefer.

1 Wash the rice until the water runs clear and then soak it for 20 minutes. Leave to drain in a colander.

2 In a heavy pan, heat the oil until it is smoking. Remove the pan from the heat and add the mustard seeds (covering the pan if necessary to prevent the mustard seeds from jumping out of the pan). Add the cinnamon, cardamom, cloves and bay leaf and let them sizzle for a few seconds.

3 Place the pan back over a medium heat and add the rice and raisins. Add the salt and sugar and cook, stirring, for 2 minutes. Pour in 450ml/16fl oz/scant 2 cups hot water and bring it to the boil. Add the lemon juice, stir and reduce the heat to low. Cover the pan tightly and cook for 7–8 minutes without lifting the lid. Switch off the heat and let the pan stand undisturbed for 8–10 minutes. Fluff up the rice with a fork and serve with Royal Corn Curry or Lentils with Spiced Butter.

Serves 4

225g/8oz/generous 1 cup basmati rice

30ml/2 tbsp mustard oil

2.5ml/½ tsp black mustard seeds

2.5cm/1in piece of cinnamon stick

4 cardamom pods, bruised

2 cloves

1 bay leaf

25g/1oz seedless raisins

5ml/1 tsp salt or to taste

5ml/1 tsp sugar

50ml/2fl oz/3 tbsp freshly squeezed lemon juice

PER PORTION Energy 294kcal/1228kJ; Protein 5.4g; Carbohydrate 52.9g, of which sugars 5.4g; Fat 6.8g, of which saturates 0.7g; Cholesterol 0mg; Calcium 28mg; Fibre 0.1g; Sodium 498mg.

Wheat-flour Flat Bread with Spiced Greens
Bathuway ki Roti

In the state of Bihar, situated near west Bengal, this fabulous spicy wheat-flour flat bread is made with locally grown greens that are difficult to get hold of anywhere else. However, you can use spinach, which makes an easy and delicious alternative. This healthy flat bread is very tasty and is the perfect accompaniment to many Indian vegetarian dishes.

Makes 10

250g/9oz spinach leaves
450g/1lb/4 cups chapati flour (atta) or fine wholemeal (whole-wheat) flour
5ml/1 tsp salt
2.5ml/½ tsp aniseeds
30ml/2 tbsp sunflower oil or plain olive oil
A little flour for dusting
Extra oil for shallow frying

1 Put the spinach in a large bowl or pan and pour over boiling water to cover it completely. Leave it to soak for 2 minutes, then drain, refresh with cold water and drain again. Squeeze out as much water as possible, but make sure that the spinach remains quite moist. Place the spinach in a food processor and chop it finely, but do not process it to a purée.

2 In a large mixing bowl, mix the flour, salt and aniseeds. Add 15ml/1 tbsp of the oil and mix well. Now, stir in the spinach, and gradually add 200ml/7fl oz/¾ cup water and mix until a soft dough is formed. You may not need all the water as the spinach leaves will release their own moisture into the flour, so add a little at a time.

3 Transfer to a flat surface, add the remaining oil and knead the dough for 3–4 minutes. Cover with a damp cloth and let it rest for 15–20 minutes.

4 Divide the dough into 2 equal parts and pinch off or cut each half into 5 equal portions. Form into balls and flatten each one into a smooth, round cake. Dust each cake in the flour and roll out to approximately an 18cm/7in circle.

5 Pre-heat a griddle over a medium heat and place a flat bread on it. Cook for 30–40 seconds and turn it over. Spread 5ml/1 tsp of oil on the surface of the bread and turn it over again. Cook until brown patches appear underneath, checking by lifting the bread with a thin spatula or a fish slice. Spread 5ml/1 tsp oil on the second side, turn it over and cook until brown patches appear. Keep the breads hot by wrapping them in a piece of foil lined with kitchen paper until they are all cooked.

PER PORTION Energy 166kcal/700kJ; Protein 6.4g; Carbohydrate 29.2g, of which sugars 1.3g; Fat 3.4g, of which saturates 0.4g; Cholesterol 0mg; Calcium 60mg; Fibre 4.6g; Sodium 36mg.

Milk Balls in Cardamom-scented Syrup

Golap Jamun

This dish is traditionally made with two dairy products known as khoya (reduced solidified milk) and chenna (cottage cheese), both of which are time-consuming to make. Full-cream milk powder or skimmed milk powder mixed with single cream are good alternatives.

1 Soak the pounded saffron in the hot milk for 10–12 minutes.

2 In a large mixing bowl, mix together the full-cream milk powder or skimmed milk powder and cream, semolina, flour, ground cardamom and baking powder. Rub in the ghee or butter. Add the milk and the saffron threads, including the milk in which they were soaked.

3 Mix until a soft dough is formed and knead it on a flat surface until smooth. Divide the dough into 2 equal parts and make 8 equal balls out of each. Rotate the balls between your palms to make them as smooth as possible, without any surface cracks.

4 Put the sugar, cardamom pods and water in a pan and bring to the boil. Stir until the sugar has dissolved. Turn the heat down and simmer the syrup for 6–8 minutes. Remove from the heat and set aside.

5 Heat the oil in a wok or other suitable pan over a low heat and deep-fry the milk balls gently until they are a rich dark brown colour. The balls will sink, but should start floating after a few minutes. If they do not float, gently ease them away from the base of the pan using a thin spatula. Turn them over carefully once or twice until they are browned all over.

6 Lift the milk balls out of the oil with a slotted spoon and lower them into the prepared syrup. Allow them to soak in the syrup while you fry the next batch. Leave them all soaking in the syrup for a couple of hours before serving.

Makes 16

5ml/1 tsp saffron threads, pounded
30ml/2 tbsp hot milk
175g/6oz/1¼ cups full-cream (whole) milk powder, or skimmed milk powder mixed with 150ml/5fl oz/½ cup single (light) cream
75g/3oz/½ cup semolina
10ml/2 tsp plain (all-purpose) flour
5ml/1 tsp ground cardamom
5ml/1 tsp baking powder
40g/1½ oz/3 tbsp ghee or unsalted butter, melted
150ml/5fl oz/½ cup milk
350g/12 oz/1¾ cups granulated (white) sugar
8 green cardamom pods, bruised
900ml/1½ pints/3½ cups water
Oil for deep frying

To serve:
Whipped double (heavy) cream mixed with 30ml/2 tbsp rose water, seasonal fresh fruits

PER PORTION Energy 219kcal/917kJ; Protein 1.6g; Carbohydrate 28.1g, of which sugars 24.6g; Fat 11.9g, of which saturates 4.1g; Cholesterol 10mg; Calcium 58mg; Fibre 0.1g; Sodium 58mg.

Serves 3–4

450ml/16fl oz/scant 2 cups water

20ml/4 tsp leaf tea, preferably Darjeeling

5–6 green cardamom pods, bruised

300ml/10fl oz/1¼ cups milk

Sugar to taste

Cook's Tip

The spiced brew can be made in advance, cooled and chilled, then re-heated as required. In the summer, the cold tea is excellent with a scoop of vanilla ice cream. We often had it as a dessert!

PER PORTION Energy 42kcal/177kJ; Protein 2.9g; Carbohydrate 4.6g, of which sugars 3.8g; Fat 1.6g, of which saturates 0.8g; Cholesterol 4mg; Calcium 95mg; Fibre 0g; Sodium 42mg.

Cardamom Tea

Cha

Spiced tea is made all over India, but the spices used vary from one region to another. North India's famous masala tea is prepared during the cold winter months with cinnamon, cardamom, cloves and sometimes ginger to induce body heat. This Bengali version has the exotic aroma of cardamom, and is rich and fragrant, rather than warming – perfect with a mid-morning snack or for afternoon tea. It also makes an excellent alternative to coffee after a meal.

1 Put the water, tea and cardamom pods into a pan and bring to the boil. Reduce the heat to low and simmer for 6–8 minutes.

2 Add the milk and increase the heat slightly. Simmer, uncovered, for 5–6 minutes until the tea has turned a pinkish-brown colour. Add more milk to taste. Remove from the heat and strain into individual cups. Add sugar to taste and serve.

south india

Chillies, coconut and curry leaves typify the cuisine of southern India. The spice region of Kerala is renowned for its sadya, a vegetarian platter consisting of an array of fabulous vegetarian dishes. The curries are light, fragrant and fresh-tasting. Onion Bhajiyas, crispy Rice Pancakes filled with Spiced Potatoes, and Cardamom-scented Soft Banana Fudge with Coconut are some of the southern snacks that are enjoyed across the length and breadth of the country.

Flavours of south India

Imagine swaying coconut palm trees, golden beaches, lush tropical scenery, temples adorned with intricate hand-crafted patterns, fine silks, precious ivory and sandalwood. This is south India, a land renowned for hectare upon hectare of tea, coffee and spice plantations and golden rice crops. Rice is the staple food throughout this region and the spices from Kerala are one of India's most prized products. The culture and culinary traditions of this region have remained intact throughout history, as this region was not subjected to foreign invasion.

The states of Andhra Pradesh and Tamil Nadu are mainly vegetarian, although rich and luxurious Mughlai-influenced meat and poultry dishes are well known in the state of Hyderabad. Pungent local chillies are used in cooking and ghee (clarified butter) and plain yogurt are served with meals as cooling aids. The cuisine in the city of Hyderabad in Andhra Pradesh has been influenced by the Muslim Royal kitchens, making it unique among the southern states. Hyderabad is famed for its fragrant biryanis and exquisite tasting kebabs.

The state of Tamil Nadu, with Madras (now Chennai) as its capital, is on the south-eastern side of the Indian peninsula. The state is renowned for production of the most exquisite silks and the preservation of age-old Indian classical dance, Bharat Natyam. It is also famed for the beautiful resort of Kanniyakumaari, and the breathtaking Blue Mountains (Nilgiri Hills) after which their most popular tea has been named. The food is fiery and emerald green banana leaves are used as dinner plates. They are filled with crispy, paper-thin rice pancakes (dosa), fluffy rice dumplings (idli) served with spicy lentils (sambhar), spicy lentil fritters (wadas) and coconut chutney.

Coastal Karnataka offers an enticing range of fish and seafood dishes cooked in coconut milk and spiced with chillies, with the distinctive flavours of curry leaves, mustard seeds and asafoetida. Some parts of this state are strictly vegetarian. Boiled rice is drizzled with ghee and served with exquisite vegetarian dishes. Raw bananas, green mango pickles, colcosia leaves and red-hot chillies are some of the ingredients used in Karnataka cooking. Bamboo shoot curry is another popular dish in this region. The famous sweetmeat of this state is Mysore pak, made with generous quantities of ghee, sugar and chickpea flour. The delicate flesh of the young, tender coconut is enjoyed as a tasty snack that is also very nutritious.

Kerala, in the southernmost tip of India, is known as the spice island due to the fabulous spice plantation, from where Indian spices are exported worldwide. It is not a vegetarian state, but has a special vegetarian banquet known as sadya, which consists of boiled rice and an array of vegetables, lentils, peas, pickles and chutneys. The meal is followed by a delicious rice dessert known as 'payasam'. Among the other vegetarian dishes are thoren (finely cut vegetables cooked in coconut oil), kalan (fruits cooked in coconut milk with chillies and curry leaves) and sweet fried bananas. Bananas, jackfruits, passion fruits and mangoes are grown locally.

Onion Bhajiyas

Kanda Bhaje

One of the most popular snacks in India, onion bhajiyas come in several versions. This south Indian recipe comes from the mainly vegetarian state of Karnataka. Bhajiyas are delicious served on their own or accompanied by a chutney of your choice.

1 Sift the flour into a large mixing bowl and add the ground rice, salt, bicarbonate of soda, turmeric, ground cumin, cumin seeds and asafoetida. Mix these dry ingredients together thoroughly, then add the chillies, onion rings and coriander. Gradually pour in 200ml/7fl oz/ ¾ cup water and mix until a thick batter is formed and all the ingredients are well coated.

2 In a wok or other suitable pan for deep-frying, heat the oil over a medium heat, ensuring the temperature reaches at least 180°C/350°F if you have a thermometer. The temperature of the oil is crucial – if it is not hot enough the bhajiyas will be soggy. To measure the temperature without a thermometer, drop about 1.5ml/¼ tsp of the batter into the hot oil. If it floats up to the surface immediately without turning brown, then the oil is at the right temperature.

3 Lower about 15ml/1 tbsp at a time of the onion batter mix into the hot oil, in a single layer. Avoid overcrowding the pan as this will lower the temperature and the bhajiyas will not crisp up.

4 Reduce the heat slightly and continue to cook until the bhajiyas are golden brown and crisp. Maintaining a steady temperature is important to ensure that the centre of each bhajiya is cooked and the outside turns brown. This should take 8–10 minutes. Drain on kitchen paper and serve the bhajiyas on their own or with a chutney of your choice.

Serves 4–6

150g/5oz/1¼ cups gram flour

25g/1oz ground rice

5ml/1 tsp salt or to taste

Pinch of bicarbonate of soda (baking soda)

2.5ml/½ tsp ground turmeric

5ml/1 tsp ground cumin

5ml/1 tsp cumin seeds

2.5ml/½ tsp asafoetida

2 green chillies, finely chopped (seeded if you like)

450g/1lb onions, sliced into half rings and separated

15g/½oz coriander (cilantro) leaves and stalks, finely chopped

Sunflower oil or plain olive oil for deep-frying

PER PORTION Energy 284kcal/1181kJ; Protein 5.1g; Carbohydrate 27g, of which sugars 4.7g; Fat 18g, of which saturates 1.9g; Cholesterol 0mg; Calcium 38mg; Fibre 3.3g; Sodium 5mg.

Makes 15

1 green (bell) pepper

1 red (bell) pepper

1 yellow (bell) pepper

200g/7oz/1¾ cups gram flour

Pinch of bicarbonate of soda (baking soda)

5ml/1 tsp fennel seeds

5ml/1 tsp cumin seeds

5ml/1 tsp coriander seeds, lightly crushed

2.5ml/½ tsp ground turmeric

3.5ml/¾ tsp salt or to taste

1–3 green chillies, finely chopped (seeded if
    you like)

Sunflower oil or plain olive oil for
    deep-frying

PER PORTION Energy 104kcal/433kJ; Protein 2.3g;
Carbohydrate 11.4g, of which sugars 2.6g; Fat 5.7g, of
which saturates 0.6g; Cholesterol 0mg; Calcium 11mg;
Fibre 1.8g; Sodium 2mg.

Batter-fried Peppers
Mirchi Bhaje

If your taste buds ever crave a change, try these irresistibly sweet
peppers, which are cut into rings, dipped in a spiced batter and
deep-fried until crisp and brown. They make a wonderful snack
at any time, or a delicious appetizer with any chutney, or a tasty
canapé piled up on a plate at drinks parties. You can use mixed
peppers or all one colour.

1 Cut the peppers into 5mm/¼in-wide rings and remove the seeds and the pith. Set aside.

2 Sift the gram flour into a mixing bowl and add all the remaining ingredients except the
oil. Mix well and gradually add 200ml/7fl oz/¾ cup water. Stir to make a thick batter.

3 Heat the oil in a wok or other suitable pan for deep-frying over a medium heat.
Dip the pepper rings, one at a time, into the spiced batter and add to the hot oil without
overcrowding the pan as this will lower the temperature of the oil and result in soggy
fritters. Fry them until they are crisp and golden brown. Drain on kitchen paper.

Rice Pancakes filled with Spiced Potatoes

Masala Dosai

Crispy rice pancakes filled with spiced potatoes and served with coconut chutney are a popular breakfast or brunch in south India. My recipe is simplified for cooks with limited time in the kitchen.

1 To make the pancakes: Mix all the dry ingredients in a large mixing bowl.

2 Beat the yogurt until smooth and blend with 450ml/16fl oz/scant 2 cups water. Gradually add the blended yogurt to the dry ingredients, beating well with a wire whisk.

3 Place a heavy non-stick griddle (23cm/9in wide) or frying pan over a medium heat and add 10ml/2 tsp oil. Brush the oil quickly all over the surface and allow to heat up for a few minutes.

4 Using a measuring jug (cup), pour approximately 125ml/4fl oz/½ cup of the batter on to the griddle, spread it quickly and evenly and let the mixture set for 2 minutes. Sprinkle 15ml/1 tbsp water around the edges, wait for 15–20 seconds, then turn the pancake over with a thin spatula or a fish slice. Cook for a further 2–3 minutes or until brown patches appear underneath. Cook the remaining pancakes the same way and place on a wire rack in a single layer.

5 For the filling: Boil the potatoes in their skins to stop them going mushy. Cool, peel and cut them into 2.5cm/1in cubes. You can cook them in advance and store them in the refrigerator.

6 Heat the oil over a medium heat. When hot, but not smoking, add the mustard seeds, followed by the cumin and fenugreek seeds. Add the onion and green chillies and stir-fry for 8–9 minutes or until the onions are a light golden colour. Add the ground turmeric, coriander and cumin. Cook for 1 minute.

7 Add the cooked potatoes and salt to the spice mixture and stir until the potatoes are heated through. Stir in the coriander leaves and remove from the heat. Divide the potato filling into 8 equal portions.

8 Place the griddle used to cook the pancakes over a low heat. Lay a cooked pancake on it, put a portion of the potato filling on one side, roll it up and heat through. Place the rolled pancakes in a very low oven while you finish making all of them, but do not leave in too long.

Makes 8

For the pancakes:

75g/3oz/⅔ cup plain (all-purpose) flour
110g/4oz/⅔ cup semolina
110g/4oz/⅔ cup ground rice
2.5ml/½ tsp salt or to taste
150g/5oz/⅔ cup natural (plain) yogurt
Sunflower oil or plain olive oil for cooking the pancakes

For the filling:

600g/1¼ lb potatoes
60ml/4 tbsp sunflower oil or plain olive oil
2.5ml/½ tsp black mustard seeds
2.5ml/½ tsp cumin seeds
1.5ml/¼ tsp fenugreek seeds
1 large onion, finely sliced
1–3 green chillies, finely chopped (seeded if you like)
2.5ml/½ tsp ground turmeric
5ml/1 tsp ground coriander
5ml/1 tsp cumin
5ml/1 tsp salt or to taste
30ml/2 tbsp coriander (cilantro) leaves, chopped

PER PORTION Energy 279kcal/1172kJ; Protein 7.1g; Carbohydrate 49.1g, of which sugars 6g; Fat 7.1g, of which saturates 1.1g; Cholesterol 0mg; Calcium 83mg; Fibre 2.2g; Sodium 29mg.

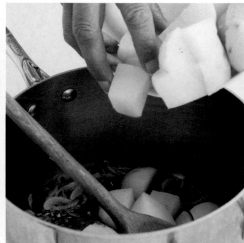

South Indian Fried Eggs

Dakshini Andey

This delicious vegetarian dish originates from Kerala and is based on a recipe known as Egg Roast. The roast is, in fact, hard-boiled eggs, fried with spices until browned. This recipe includes potatoes to make a more substantial meal. The dish can be served with any bread and a raita of your choice, and can be served on its own with a salad or as part of a complete vegetarian meal. The eggs, once 'roasted', can be used in a variety of different ways. For example, they can be quartered and used as a garnish with vegetable pilau. You can also cut them into halves and combine them with the potatoes, then sprinkle with grated cheese and place under a hot grill until melted and bubbling. All you need is a crisp green salad in order to rustle up a scrumptious meal.

Serves 4

350g/12oz potatoes

4 hard-boiled eggs

30ml/2 tbsp sunflower oil or plain olive oil

2.5ml/½ tsp ground cumin

1.5ml/¼ tsp chilli powder

1.5ml/¼ tsp ground turmeric

Salt to taste

30ml/2 tbsp coriander (cilantro) leaves, finely chopped

1 Boil the potatoes without skinning them, then cool, peel and cut them into wedges.

2 Shell the eggs and make 4 slits lengthways on each, take care not to cut them right through. Set them aside.

3 Heat the oil over a low heat in a non-stick frying pan, and add the cumin, chilli powder and turmeric, followed by the eggs. Stir them around for 2–3 minutes or until the eggs have developed a light crust. Add salt to taste and remove from the pan. Keep them hot while you fry the potatoes.

4 In the same oil, fry the potatoes over a medium heat, stirring regularly until they begin to brown. Add salt to taste.

5 Return the eggs to the pan and stir in the coriander leaves. Remove from the heat and serve.

PER PORTION Energy 199kcal/831kJ; Protein 8.5g; Carbohydrate 15.8g, of which sugars 1.1g; Fat 12g, of which saturates 2.1g; Cholesterol 190mg; Calcium 43mg; Fibre 0.9g; Sodium 81mg.

Serves 4

45ml/3 tbsp sunflower oil or plain olive oil

2.5ml/½ tsp fenugreek seeds

1–2 dried red chillies, chopped

1 large cauliflower, divided into 1cm/½in florets

400ml/14fl oz/1½ cups canned coconut milk

5ml/1 tsp salt or to taste

1 red onion, finely sliced

25ml/1½ tbsp tamarind juice or lime juice

PER PORTION Energy 153kcal/636kJ; Protein 5.9g; Carbohydrate 10.6g, of which sugars 9.5g; Fat 9.9g, of which saturates 1.5g; Cholesterol 0mg; Calcium 64mg; Fibre 2.9g; Sodium 124mg.

Cauliflower Braised with Roasted Chilli and Fenugreek

Ambat

Snow-white florets of cauliflower are simmered in rich coconut milk, teamed with lightly browned red onion and flavoured with only two spices. This dish is a classic example of the delicious, healthy cuisine of Karnataka and goes well with plain boiled or basmati rice.

1 In a small pan, heat 10ml/2 tsp of the oil over a low heat and add the fenugreek and chillies. Stir them around until they are just a shade darker. Switch off the heat and allow the spices to cool.

2 Meanwhile, blanch the cauliflower in a roomy pan for 2 minutes, drain and return to the pan. Add the coconut milk and salt. Leave it to bubble gently without a lid over a very low heat while you prepare the onion.

3 Heat the remaining oil over a medium heat and fry the onion, stirring regularly, until it begins to brown. Add the onion, together with any remaining oil in the pan, to the cauliflower mixture. Stir and increase the heat slightly.

4 Crush the fenugreek and chillies to a paste with the oil in which they were fried. Add this paste to the cauliflower along with the tamarind or lime juice. Simmer for 1–2 minutes, remove from the heat and serve with plain boiled rice.

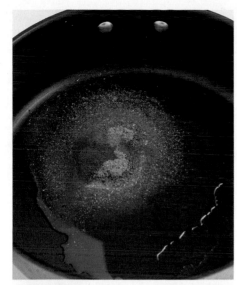

Pineapple Salad

Pachadi

Golden pineapple cubes coated with coconut and tempered with mustard, chilli and curry leaves make a delightful side dish. Although usually served as an accompaniment, it is quite easy to make a main course out of this wonderfully fragrant dish.

1 Peel the pineapple and remove the 'eyes' with a small sharp knife. Quarter the pineapple and remove the central core from each piece. Cut into 1cm/½in wedges and put into a pan with the turmeric, salt and sugar. Add 400ml/14fl oz/1½ cups water, cover and cook over a medium heat until the pineapple is tender, but still firm (12–15 minutes). Remove from the heat and leave to cool.

2 Grind the coconut in a coffee grinder and mix with the yogurt and cooked pineapple.

3 In a small pan or a steel ladle, heat the oil over a medium heat. When hot, but not smoking, add the mustard seeds, followed by the green chilli and curry leaves. Allow the seeds to crackle. Add to the pineapple mix and serve with any curry accompanied by plain boiled rice.

Serves 4

1 small pineapple

2.5ml/½ tsp ground turmeric

5ml/1 tsp salt or to taste

25g/1oz/2 tbsp white sugar

25g/1oz/⅓ cup desiccated (dry unsweetened shredded) coconut

50g/2oz/¼ cup natural (plain) yogurt

30ml/2 tbsp sunflower oil or plain olive oil

2.5ml/½ tsp black mustard seeds

1 green chilli, finely chopped (seeded if you like)

8–10 curry leaves, fresh or dried

PER PORTION Energy 160kcal/670kJ; Protein 1.4g; Carbohydrate 18g, of which sugars 18g; Fat 9.7g, of which saturates 4.1g; Cholesterol 0mg; Calcium 47mg; Fibre 2.1g; Sodium 15mg.

Potatoes in Coconut Milk with Garlic-infused Butter

Batata Ghashi

These potatoes are so fabulously tasty that you won't believe how simple they are to make. The only 'tricky' part is that you will need to pre-boil the potatoes in their skins and leave to cool completely before adding them to the sauce. Once you start scooping up these spicy coconut-drenched cubes of potato with flat bread, you'll find it hard to stop!

1 Boil the potatoes in their skins, cool and peel them and cut into 2.5cm/1in cubes.

2 Heat the oil over a low heat and add the coriander, turmeric and chilli powder. Stir and cook for about a minute. Add the potatoes, coconut milk and salt. Stir well and bring the mixture to a slow simmer. Cook gently for 6–8 minutes. Add the tamarind or lime juice.

3 Meanwhile, melt the ghee or butter over a low heat and add the garlic. Fry until it is lightly browned but do not allow it to darken. Stir the garlic butter into the potatoes, remove from the heat and serve with any bread.

Serves 4

500g/1lb 2oz potatoes (avoid floury ones)

30ml/2 tbsp sunflower oil or plain olive oil

10ml/2 tsp ground coriander

2.5ml/½ tsp ground turmeric

2.5–5ml/½–1 tsp chilli powder

400ml/14fl oz/1½ cups canned coconut milk

5ml/1 tsp salt or to taste

25ml/1½ tbsp tamarind juice or lime juice

15ml/1 tbsp ghee or unsalted butter

4–5 large garlic cloves, crushed

Cook's Tip

To reheat this dish, place the pan over a gentle heat and add 115ml/4 fl oz of warm water. Warm until it starts bubbling but do not boil as the coconut milk will split.

PER PORTION Energy 207kcal/870kJ; Protein 3.2g; Carbohydrate 26.8g, of which sugars 6.5g; Fat 10.6g, of which saturates 2.9g; Cholesterol 0mg; Calcium 46mg; Fibre 1.3g; Sodium 617mg.

Serves 4–5

75g/3oz/1 cup desiccated (dry unsweetened shredded) coconut

1–2 green chillies, chopped (seeded if you like)

2.5ml/½ tsp salt or to taste

2.5ml/½ tsp sugar

15ml/1 tbsp natural (plain) yogurt

1cm/½in piece of fresh root ginger, roughly chopped

25ml/1½ tbsp tamarind juice or lime juice

15ml/1 tbsp sunflower oil or plain olive oil

2.5ml/½ tsp black mustard seeds

6–8 curry leaves

1 dried red chilli, chopped

PER PORTION Energy 133kcal/548kJ; Protein 1.9g; Carbohydrate 4.1g, of which sugars 2g; Fat 12.3g, of which saturates 8.4g; Cholesterol 0mg; Calcium 20mg; Fibre 2.1g; Sodium 9mg.

Coconut Chutney

Thengai Thuvaiyal

In traditional Tamil Nadu style, this chutney is fiery hot. Through the pungency of the chillies, you can savour the wonderful flavour and mellow taste, with the sweet undertone of coconut and the distinctive tang of tamarind. A real explosion of flavours in your mouth! Desiccated coconut is used here, but by all means use fresh coconut if you prefer.

1 Put the coconut in a bowl and pour in enough boiling water to just cover it. Set aside for 15–20 minutes, then put into a blender. Add the green chillies, salt, sugar, yogurt, ginger and tamarind or lime juice. Blend until the ingredients are mixed to a smooth purée and transfer to a serving bowl.

2 Heat the oil in a small wok or a steel ladle over a medium heat. When hot, but not smoking, add the mustard seeds, followed by the curry leaves and red chilli. Allow the seeds to crackle and the chilli to blacken slightly, then switch off the heat. Pour the entire mixture over the chutney. Mix well and serve at room temperature.

Serves 4

225g/8oz/generous 1 cup basmati rice

25g/1oz/⅓ cup desiccated (dry unsweetened shredded) coconut

3 garlic cloves, roughly chopped

2.5cm/1in piece of fresh root ginger, roughly chopped

15g/½oz coriander (cilantro) leaves and stalks, roughly chopped

1–2 green chillies, roughly chopped (seeded if you like)

50g/2oz/4 tbsp ghee or 25g/1oz/2 tbsp unsalted butter and 30ml/2 tbsp sunflower oil or plain olive oil

25g/1oz raw cashew nuts

2.5cm/1in piece of cinnamon stick

4 cardamom pods, bruised

4 cloves

1 medium onion, finely sliced

75g/3oz/½ cup green beans, cut into 2.5cm/1in pieces

75g/3oz/½ cup peas, frozen and thawed or pre-cooked fresh

5ml/1 tsp salt or to taste

PER PORTION Energy 418kcal/1736kJ; Protein 8.2g; Carbohydrate 56g, of which sugars 5.8g; Fat 18g, of which saturates 9.4g; Cholesterol 0mg; Calcium 76mg; Fibre 3.8g; Sodium 10mg.

Pilau Rice with Coconut and Coriander Pesto

Chatni Pulao

A fabulous flavour triangle is created with fresh coriander, mint leaves and green chillies in this sumptuous pilau, which can be a vegetarian meal in itself when served with a raita. The pesto sauce used here is not dissimilar to the Italian version; however, the Indian recipe does not contain pine nuts, and the richness comes from coconut.

1 Wash the rice in several changes of water until it runs clear and then leave it to soak for 20 minutes. Drain in a colander.

2 Soak the coconut in 150ml/5fl oz/½ cup boiling water for 10 minutes, then place in a blender with the water in which it was soaked. Add the garlic, ginger, chopped coriander and chillies, and blend until smooth. Set aside.

3 Melt the ghee or butter and oil in a heavy pan over a low heat. Stir-fry the cashew nuts until browned, remove and drain on kitchen paper. In the same pan, stir-fry the cinnamon, cardamom and cloves for 30 seconds. Add the onion, increase the heat to medium and fry until the onion is golden brown, stirring regularly.

4 Add the drained rice, cook for a minute or two and add the ground coconut mixture. Stir-fry for 2–3 minutes, then add the beans, peas and salt. Pour in 450ml/16fl oz/scant 2 cups warm water, bring it to the boil, cover the pan tightly and reduce the heat to low. Cook for 8–9 minutes without lifting the lid and then switch off the heat. Let the pan stand undisturbed for 10 minutes, fluff up the rice with a fork and serve.

Coconut Rice

Thengai Sadam

This snow-white basmati rice, speckled with black mustard seeds and dotted with red chilli pieces, looks quite stunning. It is best served with a simple lentil dish or a vegetable curry.

1 Wash the rice until the water runs clear, then leave it to soak for 20 minutes. Drain and put it into a heavy pan. Pour in 450ml/16fl oz/scant 2 cups hot water. Stir in the salt and bring it to the boil. Let it boil for 2 minutes, then turn the heat down to very low, cover the pan and cook for 8 minutes without lifting the lid. Remove from the heat and let the pan stand undisturbed for 8–10 minutes.

2 Meanwhile, put the coconut into a small pan and add the milk. Stir over low to medium heat until the coconut has absorbed all the milk. This enriches the dried coconut, giving it a luscious taste.

3 Heat the oil in a small pan or a steel ladle over a low heat and brown the cashew nuts. Drain on kitchen paper. Increase the heat to medium and when the oil is fairly hot, but not smoking, add the mustard seeds, split chickpeas, red chillies and curry leaves (in that order). Allow the seeds to pop and the chillies to blacken slightly. Pour the entire contents of the pan over the rice and add the coconut and cashew nuts. Gently mix with a fork and serve.

Serves 4

225g/8oz/generous 1 cup basmati rice

5ml/1 tsp salt or to taste

50g/2oz/⅔ cup desiccated (dry unsweetened shredded) coconut

125ml/4fl oz/½ cup milk

30ml/2 tbsp sunflower oil or plain olive oil

50g/2oz/½ cup raw cashew nuts

2.5ml/½ tsp black mustard seeds

15ml/1 tbsp skinless split chickpeas (channa dhal)

2–3 dried red chillies

8–10 curry leaves

PER PORTION Energy 436kcal/1813kJ; Protein 9.3g; Carbohydrate 51.7g, of which sugars 3.1g; Fat 21.2g, of which saturates 9.4g; Cholesterol 4mg; Calcium 56mg; Fibre 2.3g; Sodium 58mg.

Rice and Wheat Pancakes

Achappam

These indulgent pancakes are enriched with coconut milk and egg. Traditionally they are made in small metal ring moulds, but you can use large moulds instead. They are delicious on their own, or you can serve them drizzled with maple syrup and fresh fruits, with Greek yogurt and clear honey, or topped with a scoop of vanilla ice cream and a coulis of fresh fruits.

1 Sift the flour into a mixing bowl and add the ground rice, sugar, cardamom and sesame seeds. Mix well.

2 Beat the eggs and gradually add the coconut milk while still beating until well blended. Pour this mixture into the flour and ground rice and mix until you have a thick batter.

3 Pour enough oil into a large frying pan to cover the base to about 1cm/½in depth and place over a low heat. Put a 5cm/2in steel ring mould in the pan and pour in enough batter to come halfway up the height of the mould. When the batter is set, after about 2–3 minutes, carefully turn it over (the top will not be completely set at this stage) and continue to cook until it is golden brown on both sides.

4 Cook all the pancakes in the same way. The cooking process will be quicker if your pan has space for 2–3 small ring moulds at the same time. Serve hot or at room temperature. The pancakes can be made in advance and chilled or frozen, and then re-heated in a moderate oven for 6–8 minutes.

Makes 18

110g/4oz/1 cup plain (all-purpose) flour

110g/4oz/⅔ cup ground rice

110g/4oz/1 cup caster (superfine) sugar

5ml/1 tsp ground cardamom

25ml/1½ tbsp sesame seeds

2 large eggs

400ml/14fl oz/1½ cups canned coconut milk

Oil for shallow frying

PER PORTION Energy 110kcal/463kJ; Protein 2.1g; Carbohydrate 17.1g, of which sugars 7.6g; Fat 4g, of which saturates 0.6g; Cholesterol 21mg; Calcium 32mg; Fibre 0.3g; Sodium 33mg.

Serves 4

2 large or 4 small mangoes

75g/3oz/1 cup desiccated (dry
  unsweetened shredded) coconut

425ml/15fl oz/1½ cups full-fat (whole) milk

5 green cardamom pods, bruised

110g/4oz palm sugar (jaggery), grated, or
  soft dark brown sugar

1.5ml/¼ tsp freshly grated nutmeg

Strawberries or other seasonal fruit

To decorate:

Sprigs of fresh mint

Mangoes in Cardamom-scented Coconut Cream

Aam ka Rasayana

This dessert is a delight for mango lovers. It is easy to make and refrigerates well for a few days. Unrefined palm sugar is traditionally used, but you could use soft dark brown sugar instead.

1 Peel the mango and slice off the two large pieces on either side of the stone, then the two thinner sides. Chop all the slices into bitesize pieces and set aside. Scrape off all the flesh next to the stone and reserve.

2 Put the coconut into a small pan and add 300ml/10fl oz/1 cup of the milk, plus the cardamom pods and sugar. Bring it to the boil, reduce the heat to low and simmer for 5 minutes. Remove from the heat and cool slightly, then purée until smooth in a blender, along with the reserved mango scrapings. Strain the coconut purée, pushing as much of the milk through the sieve (strainer) as possible. Return the solid coconut to the blender and add the remaining milk. Blend until smooth and push it through a sieve as before. Discard the solid coconut left in the sieve. Combine both the milk mixtures and add the grated nutmeg.

3 Put the chopped mango into a mixing bowl and add the sweetened, spiced coconut milk. Mix well and chill for several hours. Serve in stemmed glasses layered with sliced strawberries.

PER PORTION Energy 349kcal/1467kJ; Protein 5.3g; Carbohydrate 49.2g, of which sugars 48.8g; Fat 16g, of which saturates 12.7g; Cholesterol 15mg; Calcium 153mg; Fibre 5.2g; Sodium 67mg.

Cardamom-scented Soft Banana Fudge with Coconut

Balehannu Halwa

Halwa is the generic Indian name for any sweet cooked with sugar and a hint of spice to a soft fudge consistency. When made with freshly grated coconut and combined with the golden mashed banana, this halwa is divine. Desiccated coconut, lightly cooked in milk, works well instead of fresh coconut. The handful of chopped cashew and pistachio nuts help to provide a contrast of texture, but these can be left out if preferred. Energy-boosting bananas are rich in dietary fibre and vitamin C as well as potassium, which helps to regulate high blood pressure. They contain no fat, sodium or cholesterol.

1 Place the coconut and milk in a pan and stir over a medium heat until the coconut has absorbed all the milk. Remove from the heat and set aside. Mash the bananas with a potato masher.

2 Melt the ghee or butter over a low heat and add the mashed banana and coconut. Stir and cook for 4–5 minutes. Add the raisins, cashew nuts and sugar, and increase the heat to medium. Continue to cook, stirring all the time, for 15–17 minutes until the mixture reaches a soft fudge-like consistency.

3 Add the cardamom and grated nutmeg, and mix well.

4 Brush a 30cm/12in plate with some melted butter and spread the fudge on it, shaping it into a 15cm/6in square. Sprinkle the pistachio nuts and coconut flakes on the surface and press them down gently but firmly. Allow to cool, then chill for 2–3 hours. Cut into squares or diamonds and serve.

Serves 4–5

110g/4oz/1⅓ cups desiccated (dry unsweetened shredded) coconut

200ml/7fl oz/¾ cup full-fat (whole) milk

4–5 semi-ripe bananas

75g/3oz/6 tbsp ghee or unsalted butter

25g/1oz seedless raisins

50g/2oz raw cashew nuts, chopped (optional)

110g/4oz/1 cup granulated (white) sugar

5ml/1 tsp ground cardamom

2.5ml/½ tsp freshly grated nutmeg

25g/1oz pistachio nuts, lightly crushed (optional)

15ml/1 tbsp toasted coconut flakes

Cook's Variations

Instead of banana, ripe mango can be used in this recipe, which produces a delightfully satisfying result. Toasted sunflower seeds make a good alternative to nuts.

PER PORTION Energy 572kcal/2386kJ; Protein 6.9g; Carbohydrate 53.2g, of which sugars 49.4g; Fat 38.3g, of which saturates 21.2g; Cholesterol 6mg; Calcium 79mg; Fibre 4.8g; Sodium 89mg.

central india

An array of exciting colours, flavours and rich textures make the cuisine of central India one of the most varied and memorable experiences in the country. Crispy Gram Flour Rounds, Golden Mung Bean Patties, Turnips in a Spice-laced Yogurt Sauce, Mixed Fruits with Ginger, Cumin and Chilli, and a sweet yogurt drink are just some examples of the stunning repertoire of vegetarian cuisine from central India to be sampled and savoured here.

Central India

Madhya Pradesh is situated exactly in the centre of the country and is popularly known as the 'heart of India'. It was the largest state in India until the state of Chhattisgarh was established in 2000. It borders the states of Uttar Pradesh (northern provinces), Maharashtra, Gujarat and Rajasthan. The main cities are Bhopal, Indore and Gwalior and all three cities still have living members of Indian royalty in their palaces. The richness and luxury of the royal cuisine are still very much alive in the state today. Clove-Infused Stuffed Aubergines, Corn Kernels in Yogurt and Gram Flour Sauce and Wild Fig Kebabs are some of the examples of their vegetarian fare which are enjoyed country-wide. These dishes are often served as main meals, accompanied by lavish breads such as Ginger and Cumin-scented Puffed Bread with Spinach, or as side dishes.

The cuisine in the state varies from one region to another. Wheat grows in the northern part of the state and a variety of breads are enjoyed with spicy curries. A wheat cake known as bafla is eaten with spicy lentils and ghee (clarified butter). Rice is the staple in the southern part of the state as the climate here is ideal for growing rice. Exotic biryanis and pilaus are made with locally grown rice. However, rice is generally popular throughout the central state. Corn and milk play an important part in the vegetarian cuisine of this region, and the vast majority of the population live on a vegetarian diet. The cooking style has drawn its influences from the neighbour states of Rajasthan and Gujarat, which are both mainly vegetarian states. There is also a tribal community who have their own distinctive cusine. Among the desserts and sweetmeats, kulfi malpua (a kind of sweet dumpling) and cakes are made from a special type of locally grown wheat, known as tapu.

Although the people of Madhya Pradesh generally love desserts and sweets, such as Coconut-stuffed Parcels with Cloves, they also enjoy a variety of fruits such as creamy custard apples, juicy melons, sweet and luscious papayas, golden guavas and of course plenty of mangoes. Deliciously flavoured lassi (a yogurt based drink), almond milk and sugarcane juice are enjoyed throughout the year. Alcoholic drinks are also produced from sugarcane and date palm, as well as the juice extracted and distilled from the flowers of a local tree known as mahua.

Agriculture is the backbone of the economy of Madhya Pradesh. The main food crops are rice, wheat, sorghum and coarse millet. Flat bread made of sorghum has become popular throughout India. All types of beans, lentils and peas are grown in this area, which totals 20 per cent of the entire country's requirement. Oilseeds, cotton and sugarcane are the main commercial crops, and a significant amount of soya bean is also cultivated in this region. As well as agriculture, the state relies on forestry and mineral resources for its revenue.

Indian hospitality is renowned the world over, but the people of Madhya Pradesh are well-known throughout the country for their exceptional generosity. They follow the Indian principle of comparing a guest to God, and visitors are often overwhelmed by the lavish welcome they receive from their hosts.

Wild Fig Kebabs
Goolar Kabab

Figs are native to Asia, Africa and southern Europe and are a good source of iron and calcium. In India, wild figs are used for this recipe, but as dried figs are available all year round, I have opted for these instead, and they work extremely well. Skinless split chickpeas and figs are ground together and they combine with fresh root ginger and garlic, chillies and garam masala to produce these wonderfully fragrant kebabs.

1 Put the figs, split chickpeas, salt, ginger, garlic and onion into a pan and add 400ml/ 14fl oz/1²/₃ cups water. Bring it to the boil, reduce the heat to low and simmer, uncovered, for 25–30 minutes until the water has been absorbed. Cool slightly and add the turmeric, green chilli, chilli powder, cumin, garam masala and lemon juice. Blend the ingredients in a food processor until fine and chill for 1 hour.

2 Make the mixture into 15 equal balls and flatten each one to a neat, round cake.

3 Heat the oil in a frying pan over a medium heat and fry the kebabs on low/medium heat until they are a rich brown colour on both sides. Serve with chutney.

Makes 15

250g/9oz/1½ cups dried figs, roughly chopped

250g/9oz/1½ cups skinless split chickpeas (channa dhal)

5ml/1 tsp salt or to taste

2.5cm/1in piece of fresh root ginger, chopped

2 large garlic cloves, chopped

1 small onion, chopped

2.5ml/½ tsp ground turmeric

1 green chilli, chopped (seeded if you like)

2.5ml/½ tsp chilli powder

2.5ml/½ tsp ground cumin

2.5ml/½ tsp garam masala

Juice of 1 lemon

Sunflower oil or plain olive oil for shallow frying

PER PORTION Energy 139kcal/585kJ; Protein 5.2g; Carbohydrate 21.1g, of which sugars 10.7g; Fat 4.4g, of which saturates 0.5g; Cholesterol 0mg; Calcium 59mg; Fibre 2.5g; Sodium 17mg.

Makes 12

250g/9oz/1½ cups skinless split mung beans (mung dhal)

2.5cm/1in piece of fresh root ginger, roughly chopped

1–2 dried red chillies, chopped

5ml/1 tsp ground turmeric

15ml/1 tbsp coriander (cilantro) leaves, chopped

1 green chilli, finely chopped (seeded if you like)

50g/2oz natural (plain) yogurt

3.5ml/¾ tsp salt or to taste

Oil for deep frying

PER PORTION Energy 148kcal/620kJ; Protein 5.4g; Carbohydrate 12.6g, of which sugars 0.8g; Fat 8.9g, of which saturates 1g; Cholesterol 0mg; Calcium 22mg; Fibre 1g; Sodium 12mg.

Golden Mung Bean Patties

Mung ke Tikkia

These delicious morsels are made of skinless split mung beans that are ground to a paste and cooked with spices until the mixture reaches a mashed potato-like consistency. The mixture is then formed into small round cakes and deep-fried until crisp and golden brown. These patties have a wholesome, earthy taste and would make part of a substantial and filling meal.

1 Wash the mung beans in 2–3 changes of water and soak for 3–4 hours. Drain and put them in a food processor with the ginger and red chillies. Grind to a slightly coarse consistency, then transfer to a non-stick pan over a low heat. Add the turmeric and cook, stirring, until the mixture is dry and slightly crumbly. Remove from the heat and add all the remaining ingredients except the oil. Mix thoroughly and make 12 equal balls, then flatten them into neat, round cakes.

2 Heat the oil in a wok or other suitable pan for frying over a low/medium heat. Fry the patties until they are golden brown. Serve with any chutney.

Crispy Gram Flour Rounds

Papri

Papri is a very popular snack in central India, especially during the festival of colours (*Holi*), which is celebrated throughout the country in the spring. The predominant flavour comes from dried fenugreek. These delicious little cakes can be served on their own with drinks or used as a base for canapés with a chutney or a dip. Nutty tasting gram flour or chickpea flour is made with skinless split chickpeas by grinding the peas to a very fine powder. This extremely versatile ingredient is a rich source of protein and an excellent binding agent, and is used more commonly in vegetarian dishes such as fritters and steamed vegetable snacks. Gram flour can be stored just like regular flour.

1 In a mixing bowl, mix the gram flour, bicarbonate of soda, salt, chilli powder, cumin seeds and fenugreek leaves. Add the oil and mix well.

2 Add 125ml/4fl oz/½ cup water and mix until a dough is formed. Knead it briefly and form the dough into a large flat cake. Dust the cake with a little flour and roll it out thinly to a 30cm/12in circle about 2.5mm/⅛in thick.

3 Using a biscuit (cookie) cutter, cut out as many small circles as possible, then gather up the remaining dough and roll again. Cut out into circles as before. You should end up with about 24 small circles.

4 Heat the oil in a wok or other suitable pan for deep-frying over a medium heat. Fry the papris in hot oil in 2–3 batches until they are crisp and golden brown. Drain on kitchen paper. Once fried, they will keep well in an air-tight container for up to a week.

Serves 4

225g/8oz/2 cups gram flour, sifted
Pinch of bicarbonate of soda (baking soda)
5ml/1 tsp salt or to taste
5ml/1 tsp chilli powder
5ml/1 tsp cumin seeds
15ml/1 tbsp dried fenugreek leaves (kasuri methi)
15ml/1 tbsp sunflower oil or plain olive oil
A little flour for dusting
Oil for deep frying

Cook's Variation

To vary the taste, use finely chopped green chilli and fresh coriander (cilantro) leaves, instead of fenugreek and chilli powder.

PER PORTION Energy 358kcal/1498kJ; Protein 7.7g; Carbohydrate 37.3g, of which sugars 1.2g; Fat 21g, of which saturates 2.6g; Cholesterol 0mg; Calcium 28mg; Fibre 5.1g; Sodium 3mg.

Mung Beans with Mustard Paste, Ginger and Yogurt

Khatte Sabut Mung

This is a relatively easy dish to make, as well as being a very healthy one. Dark green mung beans with flecks of red chillies, spiced with mustard, fresh root ginger and cumin, and a creamy yogurt sauce offer plenty of visual appeal and a tantalizing taste. Mung beans are readily available in supermarkets, health-food shops and Asian stores. The sauce is made with just yogurt, with no added water or stock. It is important to whisk the yogurt well beforehand to prevent it curdling during cooking. Use relatively moisture-free, natural yogurt, such as Greek, if possible.

1 Wash and drain the mung beans and soak them for 6–8 hours or overnight.

2 Drain the beans and put them in a pan with 450ml/15fl oz/scant 2 cups water. Bring it to the boil and skim off the froth from the surface.

3 Cook the beans on a medium heat for 12–15 minutes. Stir gently as the water evaporates, reduce the heat to low and cook for 5 minutes longer. The beans should remain whole and approximately 30–45ml/2–3 tbsp liquid should remain. Remove from the heat and set aside.

4 Heat the oil over a medium heat and add the cumin seeds and red chillies. Allow the chillies to blacken. Add the onion, ginger and green chilli, and stir-fry until the onion begins to brown. Add the turmeric, salt and the cooked beans.

5 Whisk the yogurt until smooth and add to the bean mixture. Reduce the heat to low, add the mustard paste and cook for 4–5 minutes. Stir in the lime juice and remove from the heat. Serve with Ginger and Cumin-flavoured Puffed Bread with Spinach.

Serves 4

225g/8oz/1¼ cups mung beans
60ml/4 tbsp sunflower oil or plain olive oil
5ml/1 tsp cumin seeds
2 whole dried red chillies
1 medium onion, finely chopped
2.5cm/1in piece of fresh root ginger, grated
1 green chilli, finely chopped (seeded if you like)
2.5ml/½ tsp ground turmeric
5ml/1 tsp salt or to taste
200g/7oz/scant 1 cup Greek (US strained plain) yogurt
15ml/1 tbsp English mustard paste
15ml/1 tbsp lime juice

PER PORTION Energy 334kcal/1403kJ; Protein 17.3g; Carbohydrate 39.1g, of which sugars 10.8g; Fat 13.5g, of which saturates 1.8g; Cholesterol 1mg; Calcium 190mg; Fibre 10.2g; Sodium 57mg.

Corn Kernels in Yogurt and Gram Flour Sauce

Makki ke Dane ki Kari

Golden gram flour sauce, spiced with cumin and coriander and accentuated with chillies, mingles with the sweet, milky taste of the corn kernels to create this enticing dish. Canned corn kernels can be used instead of frozen, but drain and rinse them well beforehand. Serve with Ginger and Cumin-scented Puffed Bread with Spinach or Butter-flavoured Rice with Spice-infused Stock for a fabulous meal. Plain naan is also ideal to mop up the delicious sauce.

1 Whisk the yogurt and gram flour together and set aside.

2 Heat the oil over a medium heat and add the mustard seeds. As soon as they begin to pop, add the cumin seeds and let them sizzle for a few seconds.

3 Add the onion and stir-fry until translucent (5–6 minutes). Add the ginger and garlic and stir-fry for about a minute.

4 Reduce the heat to low and add the coriander, turmeric and chilli powder. Fry gently for 30–40 seconds, then add the yogurt mixture and cook for 3–4 minutes, stirring constantly.

5 Add the corn, salt and 200ml/7fl oz/¾ cup warm water. Cook until the sauce begins to bubble, cover the pan and simmer over a low heat for 15–20 minutes.

6 In a small pan or a steel ladle, melt the ghee or butter over a low heat and add the garam masala. Stir and cook for about 30 seconds, then pour the spiced butter over the corn, making sure that none of the garam masala is left behind.

7 Stir in the coriander leaves and remove from the heat. Pour into a serving dish and garnish with julienne strips of tomato.

Serves 4

150g/5oz/⅔ cup full-fat (whole) natural (plain) yogurt
30ml/2 tbsp gram flour, sifted
45ml/3 tbsp sunflower oil or plain olive oil
2.5ml/½ tsp black mustard seeds
2.5ml/½ tsp cumin seeds
1 medium onion, finely chopped
5ml/1 tsp ginger purée
5ml/1 tsp garlic purée
10ml/2 tsp ground coriander
2.5ml/½ tsp ground turmeric
2.5–5ml/½–1 tsp chilli powder
400g/14oz/2¼ cups frozen corn, thawed
5ml/1 tsp salt or to taste
10ml/2 tsp ghee or unsalted butter
2.5ml/½ tsp garam masala
30ml/2 tbsp coriander (cilantro) leaves, finely chopped

To garnish:
Julienne strips of fresh tomato

PER PORTION Energy 258kcal/1068kJ; Protein 6.9g; Carbohydrate 16.7g, of which sugars 7.6g; Fat 18.7g, of which saturates 5.6g; Cholesterol 5mg; Calcium 84mg; Fibre 3.2g; Sodium 1165mg.

Clove-infused Stuffed Aubergines

Baingan ke Lonj

Small, slim aubergines are used in this traditional dish. The aubergines are sliced from the top down to the stem without cutting them right through, and a spicy onion paste tempered with clove and cinnamon is spread between the slices, before they are gently simmered. This dish goes well with rice or lentils.

1 Trim off the stalks from the aubergines. Cut the aubergines lengthways from the top down to the stem without cutting them right through, leaving about 5mm/¼in uncut at the stem end. Soak them in plenty of salted water for 15–20 minutes.

2 Meanwhile, heat half the oil over a medium heat and add the onion, ginger and chillies. Stir-fry for 4–5 minutes until the onion is soft. Reduce the heat to low and add half the salt, plus the turmeric, chilli powder, coriander and cumin. Cook for 1 minute, stir in the garam masala and remove from the heat.

3 Drain the aubergines, rinse and dry them with a cloth. Stuff them with the onion mixture, using about 5ml/1 tsp of mixture per aubergine, and tie them up with a piece of thread in a criss-cross fashion. Reserve any remaining onion mixture.

4 Heat the remaining oil in a large pan over a low heat and add the cloves and cinnamon. Let them sizzle for a few seconds, then add the stuffed aubergines and the remaining salt.

5 Increase the heat to medium and cook the aubergines, stirring, for 3–4 minutes. Add any reserved onion mixture and pour in 500ml/18fl oz/2 cups warm water. Bring it to the boil, reduce the heat to low, cover the pan and cook for 20 minutes.

6 At the end of the cooking time, remove the lid and cook uncovered for a few minutes longer, if necessary, to reduce the sauce. There should be very little liquid left and the thickened spice paste should coat the aubergines. Remove from the heat and discard the threads. Serve with rice and/or phulkas and a lentil dish.

Serves 4

400g/14oz small, slim aubergines (eggplants)
60ml/4 tbsp sunflower oil or plain olive oil
1 large onion, finely chopped
10ml/2 tsp ginger purée
1–2 green chillies, finely chopped (seeded if you like)
5ml/1 tsp salt or to taste
5ml/1 tsp ground turmeric
2.5ml/½ tsp chilli powder
5ml/1 tsp ground coriander
2.5ml/½ tsp ground cumin
2.5ml/½ tsp garam masala
4 cloves
1cm/½in piece of cinnamon stick

To garnish:
Julienne strips of fresh tomato and sprigs of coriander (cilantro)

Also needed:
Natural cotton sewing thread (if using)

PER PORTION Energy 188kcal/779kJ; Protein 3.9g; Carbohydrate 15.6g, of which sugars 9g; Fat 13g, of which saturates 1.6g; Cholesterol 0mg; Calcium 59mg; Fibre 3.8g; Sodium 9mg.

Turnips in a Spice-laced Yogurt Sauce
Shalgam ka Salan

Fresh turnips are readily available in supermarkets throughout the year. Try to find the small ones as they have a delicate flavour with a slightly sweet taste which complements the sour-hot yogurt sauce. As a vegetarian main course this merits the use of ghee, which enriches the dish, but you could use oil instead if you prefer. Avoid using unsalted butter, though, as the initial cooking temperature is fairly high. You can prepare this dish in advance by cooking up to the end of step 4. Then, when ready to eat, simply complete step 5.

1 Peel the turnips and quarter them. Cut each quarter into 4 small pieces. Peel and cut the potatoes to the same size as the turnips.

2 Whisk the yogurt and gram flour together and set aside.

3 Heat half the ghee over a medium/high heat and brown the turnips, stirring them frequently, until they have a very light crust. Drain on kitchen paper. Brown the potatoes in the same way and drain.

4 Add the remaining ghee, and reduce the heat to low/medium. Fry the onion, ginger and green chillies until the onion is golden brown. Add the coriander, cumin, chilli powder and turmeric, and cook for about a minute. Add the browned vegetables and the yogurt and flour mixture.

5 Add the salt, sugar and 50ml/2fl oz/3 tbsp water. Reduce the heat to low, cover the pan and cook for 20 minutes, stirring and re-positioning the vegetables 3–4 times. Sprinkle over the garam masala and coriander leaves, stir and remove from the heat. Serve with any Indian bread.

Serves 4

5–6 turnips (about 600g/1¼lb)

275g/10oz potatoes

115g/4oz/½ cup full-fat (whole) natural (plain) yogurt

10ml/2 tsp gram flour, sifted

50g/2oz ghee

1 large onion, finely sliced

10ml/2 tsp ginger purée

1–2 green chillies, finely chopped (seeded if you like)

5ml/1 tsp ground coriander

2.5ml/½ tsp ground cumin

2.5ml/½ tsp chilli powder

2.5ml/½ tsp ground turmeric

5ml/1 tsp salt or to taste

2.5ml/½ tsp sugar

2.5ml/½ tsp garam masala

30ml/2 tbsp coriander (cilantro) leaves, finely chopped

PER PORTION Energy 317kcal/1326kJ; Protein 7.9g; Carbohydrate 39.6g, of which sugars 17g; Fat 15.6g, of which saturates 6.7g; Cholesterol 3mg; Calcium 194mg; Fibre 6.3g; Sodium 61mg.

Mixed Fruits with Ginger, Cumin and Chilli

Phalon ka Chaat

Fresh mixed fruits, lightly dusted with spices, can be enjoyed as a side dish or after dinner instead of a dessert. Any combination of fruits will work well, depending on the season, but this recipe uses three sun-kissed tropical fruits that have fantastic health benefits and are also easily available in supermarkets all year round. Papaya, or pawpaw, has a sweet, buttery taste and is reported to contain high anti-oxidant levels. The juicy pomegranate is also rich in anti-oxidants, while pineapples are known to have anti-inflammatory as well as anti-oxidant properties.

1 Using the handle of a large knife, tap the pomegranate all around. This loosens the seeds inside, making it easier to remove them.

2 Cut the pomegranate in half and remove the seeds by peeling off the outer skin as you would an orange. Remove the white pith and skin next to the seeds and reserve the seeds.

3 Peel the papaya. Cut it in half lengthwise and remove the black seeds. Scrape off the white pith under the seeds and cut the fruit into 2.5cm/1in cubes.

4 Peel the pineapple, remove the eyes with a small sharp knife and cut into quarters. Remove the hard central core and cut the pineapple into bitesize pieces.

5 Halve the grapes. Mix all the prepared fruits together in a large bowl. Add the rest of the ingredients, except the salt, and mix them thoroughly. Chill for 1–2 hours.

6 Stir in the salt and serve, garnished with the sprigs of mint, for a refreshing fruit salad

Serves 4

1 ripe pomegranate
1 ripe papaya
1 small or ½ medium pineapple
175g/6oz/1½ cups seedless green grapes
175g/6oz/1½ cups seedless black grapes
2.5ml/½ tsp ground ginger
1.5ml/¼ tsp ground black pepper
2.5ml/½ tsp ground cumin
Pinch of chilli powder
2.5ml/½ tsp dried mint or 6–8 fresh mint leaves, finely chopped
2.5ml/½ tsp sugar
2.5ml/½ tsp salt

To garnish:
Fresh mint sprigs

PER PORTION Energy 167kcal/714kJ; Protein 2.2g; Carbohydrate 40.3g, of which sugars 30g; Fat 1g, of which saturates 0.1g; Cholesterol 0mg; Calcium 77mg; Fibre 5.7g, Sodium 14mg.

New Potatoes in Yogurt and Poppy Seed Sauce

Dum Aloo

This is a rich side dish, which can also be served as a main course with any Indian bread. The potatoes are boiled first, but not fully cooked, then combined with a purée of yogurt, poppy seeds and fried onions. The final cooking is done using the *dum* (steam cooking) method, using a well-sealed pan and very gentle heat, either on the stove or in a low oven.

1 Grind the poppy seeds in a coffee grinder and set aside.

2 In a heavy pan, heat the oil over a medium heat and fry the potatoes in two batches until they are well browned. Drain them on kitchen paper. When they are cool enough to handle, prick the potatoes all over with a skewer to allow the flavours to penetrate.

3 In the same oil, fry the onion until it is a pale golden colour. Press the onion to the side of the pan to remove any excess oil and drain on kitchen paper. Blend the yogurt, poppy seeds and fried onion in a blender to form a smooth purée and set aside.

4 In the remaining oil in the pan, fry the ginger over a low heat for about a minute and add the chilli powder, coriander and cumin. Stir-fry for 30–40 seconds and add the purée.

5 Cook until the mixture begins to bubble, then add the browned potatoes, salt and garam masala. Cover the pan with a piece of foil and seal the edges by pressing the foil all the way round the edge. Put the lid on and reduce the heat to very low.

6 Cook until the potatoes are tender and the sauce has thickened – about 30 minutes. Remove from the heat and serve with any Indian bread. If you prefer to use the oven, pre-heat it to 160°C/325°F/Gas 3 and cook the potatoes in a well-sealed dish in the centre of the oven for 35–40 minutes.

Serves 4

15ml/1 tbsp white poppy seeds

60ml/4 tbsp sunflower oil or plain olive oil

700g/1½lb new potatoes, par-boiled and peeled

1 large onion, finely sliced

75g/3oz/⅓ cup full-fat (whole) natural (plain) yogurt

5ml/1 tsp ginger purée

2.5–5ml/½–1 tsp chilli powder

5ml/1 tsp ground coriander

5ml/1 tsp ground cumin

5ml/1 tsp salt or to taste

2.5ml/½ tsp garam masala

PER PORTION Energy 322kcal/1346kJ; Protein 7.2g; Carbohydrate 41.7g, of which sugars 10.8g; Fat 15.3g, of which saturates 2.3g; Cholesterol 2mg; Calcium 116mg; Fibre 3.8g; Sodium 41mg.

Ginger- and Cumin-scented Puffed Bread with Spinach

Palak Puri

This delectable bread from the Indore area is gently aromatic and its flavours mingle happily with any vegetable curry. Traditionally, the dough is divided into small portions and each puri is rolled out individually, but in order to save time, you can roll out larger portions and cut them into smaller circles with a metal cutter.

1 Put the spinach in a heatproof bowl and pour over enough boiling water to cover. Stir to ensure that all the leaves are immersed in the water. Leave them soaking for 2 minutes, then drain and refresh in cold water. Squeeze out excess water from the spinach and chop the leaves finely with a large knife or in a food processor.

2 Put the flour in a mixing bowl and add the aniseed, salt, ginger and chilli powder. Mix well and rub in the butter or margarine. Add the chopped spinach and 30ml/1fl oz/ 30ml/2 tbsp water, and mix until a soft dough is formed. Transfer the dough to a flat surface and knead for 3–4 minutes. Cover with a damp cloth and set aside for 30 minutes.

3 Divide the dough into 2 equal parts and pinch off or cut 10 equal portions from each. Form into balls and flatten to smooth, round cakes. Dust the cakes lightly in flour and roll each one out to a 7.5cm/3in circle, taking care not to tear or pierce them as they will not puff up if damaged. Place them in a single layer on a piece of baking parchment and cover with another piece of parchment.

4 Heat the oil in a wok or other pan suitable for deep-frying. When the oil has a faint shimmer of rising smoke on the surface, carefully drop in one puri. As soon as it rises to the surface, gently tap round the edges to encourage puffing. When it has puffed up, turn it over and fry the other side until browned. Drain on kitchen paper. Keep the fried puris on a baking tray in a single layer. They are best eaten fresh, though they can be re-heated briefly for 2–3 minutes in a hot oven. Serve with any vegetable curry.

Makes 20

100g/3½oz fresh spinach leaves

300g/10oz/2½ cups chapati flour (atta) or fine wholemeal (whole-wheat) flour

2.5ml/½ tsp aniseed

2.5ml/½ tsp salt

5ml/1 tsp ginger purée

2.5ml/½ tsp chilli powder

25g/1oz butter or margarine

30ml/1fl oz/2 tbsp water

Flour for dusting

Oil for deep-frying

PER PORTION Energy 58kcal/247kJ; Protein 2.1g; Carbohydrate 9.8g, of which sugars 0.4g; Fat 1.5g, of which saturates 0.7g; Cholesterol 3mg; Calcium 15mg; Fibre 1.5g; Sodium 17mg.

Makes 8

400g/14oz/3½ cups gram flour, sifted

5ml/1 tsp nigella seeds

1.5ml/¼ tsp asafoetida

5ml/1 tsp salt or to taste

1 medium onion, grated

1 green chilli, finely chopped (seeded if you like)

45ml/3 tbsp coriander (cilantro) leaves, finely chopped

Gram flour for dusting

Oil for cooking

PER PORTION Energy 237kcal/1002kJ; Protein 4.5g; Carbohydrate 39.2g, of which sugars 0.4g; Fat 8.1g, of which saturates 0.9g; Cholesterol 0mg; Calcium 21mg; Fibre 6g; Sodium 1mg.

Spiced Gram Flour Flat Bread

Besan ki Roti

This bread is ideal for anyone who needs to avoid gluten. Gram flour is kneaded together with grated onion, asafoetida and chillies. The bread is then griddle-roasted, which gives a delicious toasted aroma and a nutty taste. You can spread a little butter on the surface of the cooked bread to give it a more moist texture.

1 Put the gram flour in a mixing bowl and add the nigella seeds, asafoetida and salt. Mix well, then add the onion, green chilli and chopped coriander and mix until all the ingredients are well blended. Gradually add 100ml/3½fl oz/7 tbsp water until a dough forms.

2 Transfer the dough to a flat surface and knead it for a couple of minutes with gentle pressure, turning it around frequently. If the dough sticks to your fingers, add a little oil. Divide the dough into 8 equal portions and flatten them into round cakes. Dust each cake in the flour and roll them out to circles of about 13cm/5in diameter.

3 Preheat a griddle over a low/medium heat and place a flat bread on it. Cook it for about a minute and then spread 15ml/1 tbsp oil around the edges. Continue to cook for a further 30–40 seconds or until browned. Turn the bread over and cook the second side until browned.

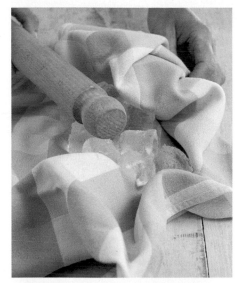

Sweet Yogurt Drink

Meethi Lassi

Lassi originated in the northern state of Punjab and quickly became a favourite drink of the entire nation. The people of northern India favour savoury lassi, but those in central India are very partial to all things sweet. This is a basic sweet lassi recipe which you can vary by using other flavourings such as vanilla, orange or mango instead of rose water. Teetotallers enjoy it, others use it as a cure for hangovers and vegetarians thrive on it!

1 Put the yogurt and sugar in a blender and add 600ml/1 pint/2½ cups water. Blend until smooth. Taste and add more sugar if necessary. Pour into a jug and chill for several hours.

2 Stir in the rose water and serve in tall glasses lined with crushed ice.

Serves 4

450g/1lb/2 cups natural (plain) yogurt

75g/3oz/⅔ cup caster (superfine) sugar

30ml/2 tbsp rose water

Fresh rose petals, to decorate

Cook's Tip

Use whole-milk yogurt, which closely resembles the home-made Indian version in terms of taste and texture.

PER PORTION Energy 137kcal/581kJ; Protein 5.8g; Carbohydrate 28g, of which sugars 28g; Fat 1.1g, of which saturates 0.6g; Cholesterol 1mg; Calcium 224mg; Fibre 0g; Sodium 95mg.

Coconut-stuffed Parcels with Cloves

Lavang Lata

The people of central India love desserts and sweetmeats. Lavang lata is a pretty parcel of cardamom-scented coconut wrapped in a simple, home-made pastry with a whole clove to hold the parcel together. These delicious morsels are ideal with a cup of tea or after dinner with coffee instead of a dessert.

1 First make the pastry. Sift the flour into a mixing bowl and rub in the ghee or butter. Mix until the flour looks crumbly. Gradually add the water and mix until a soft dough is formed. Transfer to a flat surface and knead it until it is smooth and pliable. Cover with clear film (plastic wrap) and allow to rest for 30 minutes.

2 Meanwhile, mix all the ingredients for the filling and set aside.

3 Put all the syrup ingredients together in a pan and place over a high heat. Bring to the boil, then reduce the heat to low. Simmer for 10–12 minutes and switch off the heat.

4 Divide the dough into 12 equal parts and make a neat, round cake out of each portion. Roll each one into a 7.5cm/3in circle. Divide the filling into 12 equal parts and place one portion in the centre of each circle. Enclose the filling by folding over all four corners to form a square. Secure with a clove.

5 Heat the oil for deep-frying over a low/medium heat and fry the coconut parcels in 2–3 batches until they are crisp and golden brown. Immerse immediately in the hot syrup (re-heat syrup gently if necessary). Spoon some of the syrup over the top of the parcels and leave them immersed until you have finished frying the next batch.

6 Remove the first batch from the syrup and place them in a serving dish, then immerse the second batch in the syrup, spooning over some of the syrup as before. When you have taken the last batch out of the syrup, boil the remaining syrup and reduce it to half. Spoon the thickened syrup over the parcels and serve at room temperature.

Makes 12

For the pastry:
225g/8oz/2 cups plain (all-purpose) flour
40g/1½oz/3 tbsp ghee or butter
125ml/4fl oz/½ cup cold water
Extra flour for dusting
12 whole cloves
Oil for deep-frying

For the filling:
50g/2oz/⅔ cup desiccated (dry unsweetened shredded) coconut
75ml/3fl oz/5 tbsp hot milk
50g/2oz seedless raisins
50g/2oz raw cashew nuts, chopped
5ml/1 tsp ground cardamom
2.5ml/½ tsp ground nutmeg

For the syrup:
175g/6oz/scant 1 cup granulated (white) sugar
5 cardamom pods, bruised
300ml/10fl oz/1¼ cups water

PER PORTION Energy 267kcal/1118kJ; Protein 3.2g; Carbohydrate 34.1g, of which sugars 19.2g; Fat 14g, of which saturates 5g; Cholesterol 1mg; Calcium 46mg; Fibre 1.4g; Sodium 21mg.

west india

The food of western India has stunning visual appeal, tastes beautifully aromatic, and is wholesome and healthy. Vegetarian food dominates the daily diet in this region, with meat and fish being eaten in limited quantities. Thick and creamy home-made yogurt and cheese are used in everyday cooking. Chilli-hot food sits in perfect harmony with rich coconut milk, tangy tamarind juice, silky-smooth yogurt and buttermilk.

Flavours of west India

Western India has a breathtaking variety of landscapes, with contrasts provided by tidal mudflats, steep ravines and numerous beautiful beaches. The coastal lowland, broken up by hills and short rivers, coconut palm trees and paddy fields, creates stunning vistas. The vast coastline produces an abundance of fish and seafood. Coconut milk and coconut oil are generally used in everyday cooking. Groundnut (peanut) oil is also produced and used in cooking. Both rice and wheat are grown extensively in the area.

Distinctly different types of cuisine are prevalent throughout western India. In Goa, for example, Muslims, Hindus and Christians have their own preferred ingredients and cooking styles. Mumbai (formerly Bombay) is known for its world-famous dhansak dishes as well as the unique and inimitable Parsi cuisine.

Rajasthan, Gujarat, Maharashtra and Goa are the four states in western India. Gujarat and Maharashtra are mainly vegetarian. Gujarat, on the banks of the Arabian Sea, was a refuge for the ancient Persians who fled their country. Persian-influenced dhansak is one of the region's most famous dishes. The Portuguese also landed in Gujarat before moving further west to Goa. They contributed numerous meat, poultry and seafood dishes, although the native Gujaratis are strict vegetarians. They have truly perfected the art of vegetarian cooking. The famous *thali* (a meal served on a steel platter) originated in Gujarat. Gujarati rotli, an unleavened flat bread, and cumin-flavoured lassi, a diluted yogurt drink, are very popular. Gujarati snacks, known as farsan, are famous all over the country.

Maharashtra has its own distinct cuisine based on beans, peas, lentils, wheat and fresh vegetables. Mumbai, the capital of Maharashtra, has a potpourri of food from the different communities who live there. The city of Pune is the heart of Maharashtra's vegetarian food culture. Leafy and root vegetables, lentils, peas and beans are cooked in groundnut oil, as well as an extensive range of spicy gram flour snacks, including the famous onion bhajiya. Peanuts and cashew nuts are used commonly in cooking.

Rajasthan is home to maharajas (emperors) and rajputs (princes). Royal presence ensured exquisite game, meat, poultry and fish dishes as well as delectable vegetarian fare. Although the desert climate does not encourage much in the way of vegetation, produce is sun-dried during the summer and preserved for the remaining seasons.

The state of Goa is popularly known as Golden Goa and as the Pearl of the Orient, and has a rich history and tapestry of cultures. Goa was ruled, in turn, by the Hindus, the Muslims, followed by the Portuguese. It is the only state where people belonging to different religions live in complete harmony, respecting each other's social and religious customs. Goan food is a fabulous blend of east and west as a result of the Portuguese influence. Vindaloo is Goa's most famous export. Goa may be a very small state, but the magnificent range of food that it offers is virtually unmatched.

Split Chickpea Squares in Coconut and Coriander Dressing

Amiri Khaman

This simple, delicious and highly nutritious dish comes from the mainly vegetarian state of Gujarat, which is well known for its deliciously spiced snacks, known as farsan. Every Gujarati housewife has a supply of home-made farsan in the store cupboard, which helps them to follow the age-old Indian custom of looking after their guests, whether invited or unexpected. These wonderfully aromatic squares make fabulous appetizers when served with chutney, for afternoon tea or party snacks.

1 Wash the chickpeas and soak in cold water for 5–6 hours or overnight. Drain and process in a food processor until a fine paste is formed.

2 In a wok or non-stick pan, heat the oil over a medium heat. When hot, but not smoking, add the mustard seeds and reduce the heat to low.

3 Add the asafoetida, followed by the ginger, garlic, chillies and turmeric. Fry them gently for about a minute. Add the chickpea paste, salt and sugar, and cook over a medium/low heat, stirring constantly, until the mixture is completely dry and looks crumbly.

4 Add one-third of the milk and continue to cook, stirring, for 3–4 minutes. Repeat the process with the remaining milk.

5 Add the lemon juice and stir until well blended. Spread the mixture on a lightly greased plate to a 30cm/12in rectangle and sprinkle over the coriander and coconut, pressing them down gently so that they stick to the chickpea mixture. Cut into squares or diamonds and serve hot or cold.

Serves 4–5

- 350g/12oz/2 cups skinless split chickpeas (channa dhal)
- 45ml/3 tbsp sunflower oil or light olive oil
- 2.5ml/½ tsp black mustard seeds
- 1.5ml/¼ tsp asafoetida
- 10ml/2 tsp ginger purée
- 10ml/2 tsp garlic purée
- 2–4 green chillies, finely chopped (seeded if you like)
- 2.5ml/½ tsp ground turmeric
- 5ml/1 tsp salt or to taste
- 5ml/1 tsp sugar
- 425ml/¾ pint/1¾ cups full-fat (whole) milk
- 30ml/2 tbsp lemon juice
- 15ml/1 tbsp coriander (cilantro) leaves, finely chopped
- 15ml/1 tbsp desiccated (dry unsweetened shredded) coconut

PER PORTION Energy 357kcal/1499kJ; Protein 18.5g; Carbohydrate 40.9g, of which sugars 5.9g; Fat 14.5g, of which saturates 3.3g; Cholesterol 12mg; Calcium 221mg; Fibre 7.5g; Sodium 76mg.

Spiced Gram Flour Dumplings with Fenugreek

Methi Na Muthia

In this recipe, a golden gram flour mixture binds the fenugreek leaves, and the mixture is then made into small dumplings and steamed. It is the final tempering with whole spices, curry leaves and chillies that really brings the dumplings to life.

1 Sift the gram flour into a mixing bowl and add all the remaining dumpling ingredients except the lime juice and oil. Mix thoroughly, then add the lime juice and warmed oil, and mix again. Add 100ml/3½fl oz/⅓ cup cold water and mix until a dough is formed.

2 Divide the dough into 4 equal portions and roll each one into a cylinder shape 8cm/3¼in long. Place them in a steamer and cook for 15–16 minutes. Remove from the heat, transfer them on to a cutting board and leave to cool a little. Cut the cylinders into 1cm/½in-thick slices and put them in a serving dish.

3 Heat the oil for the tempering in a small pan or steel ladle over a medium heat. When hot, but not smoking, add the mustard seeds. As soon as they pop, add the cumin, asafoetida and curry leaves. Let them sizzle for 10–15 seconds, then pour the spiced oil, along with all the whole spices, over the dumplings. Add the coriander leaves, mix well and serve immediately.

Serves 4

For the dumplings:

300g/10½oz/2½ cups gram flour

30ml/2 tbsp dried fenugreek leaves (kasuri methi)

1.5ml/¼ tsp bicarbonate of soda (baking soda)

1.5ml/¼ tsp asafoetida

2.5ml/½ tsp chilli powder

2.5ml/½ tsp ground turmeric

3.5ml/¾ tsp salt or to taste

Juice of 1 lime

30ml/2 tbsp sunflower oil or plain olive oil, warmed

For the tempering:

30ml/2 tbsp sunflower oil or plain olive oil

2.5ml/½ tsp black mustard seeds

2.5ml/½ tsp cumin seeds

1.5ml/¼ tsp asafoetida

8–10 curry leaves

30ml/2 tbsp coriander (cilantro) leaves, finely chopped

PER PORTION Energy 285kcal/1201kJ; Protein 8.7g; Carbohydrate 40.8g, of which sugars 1.3g; Fat 11g, of which saturates 1.4g; Cholesterol 0mg; Calcium 35mg; Fibre 5.4g; Sodium 4mg.

Serves 4

700g/1½lb potatoes

60ml/4 tbsp sunflower oil or plain olive oil

1 medium onion, finely chopped

1–2 green chillies, finely chopped (seeded if you like)

5ml/1 tsp salt or to taste

15g/½oz coriander (cilantro) leaves and stalks, finely chopped

4 large eggs

1.5ml/¼ tsp chilli powder or paprika

1.5ml/¼ tsp ground cumin

PER PORTION Energy 303kcal/1270kJ; Protein 9.6g; Carbohydrate 29.7g, of which sugars 3.2g; Fat 17.2g, of which saturates 3.1g; Cholesterol 190mg; Calcium 52mg; Fibre 2.2g; Sodium 91mg.

Eggs on Spiced Potatoes
Sali Pur Eeda

The inspiration for this recipe comes from the wonderful culinary repertoire of the Parsis, a people who migrated to India centuries ago from their homeland in Persia. This is a healthier version of the original recipe as the potatoes are shallow-fried rather than deep-fried.

1 Peel the potatoes and slice them thinly. Cut the slices into strips about the size of thin French fries. Wash the potatoes and dry thoroughly with a clean cloth.

2 In a non-stick sauté pan with a lid, heat the oil over a medium heat and fry the onion and chillies for 5–6 minutes, until the onions begin to brown.

3 Add the potatoes and salt. Stir and mix well, then cover the pan and cook for 10–12 minutes. Stir occasionally and reduce the heat for the last 2–3 minutes. The potatoes should brown slightly.

4 Stir in the coriander leaves and smooth the surface by gently pressing down the potatoes.

5 Break the eggs on top of the potatoes, spacing them out evenly. Reduce the heat to low, cover the pan and cook for 6–7 minutes or until the eggs are set. Remove the pan from the heat and sprinkle the chilli powder or paprika and cumin over the surface. Serve with a wide spatula or fish slice so that you can pick up a portion of potato and one egg together. Serve with chapatis or pooris.

Crispy Vegetable Triangles

Vegetable Samosas

The original recipe for samosas is a vegetarian one. Potatoes and garden peas are the most common fillings, but other vegetables such as carrots and cauliflower are also used in some regions. Filo pastry is a quick and easy alternative to traditional Indian pastry, and makes a delicious samosa that is also lower in fat. These samosas have been baked in the oven, but they can also be deep-fried in a light cooking oil such as sunflower.

1 Heat the oil over a medium heat. When it is hot but not smoking, add the asafoetida, followed by the mustard, cumin, and nigella seeds. Add the onion and green chillies and fry until the onion is beginning to brown.

2 Add the turmeric and cumin, cook for about a minute, then add the potatoes, peas, carrots and salt. Stir them around until the vegetables are thoroughly coated with the spices. Stir in the coriander leaves and remove from the heat. Allow the mixture to cool completely.

3 Pre-heat the oven to 180°C/350°F/Gas 4 and line a baking sheet with greased baking parchment.

4 Remove the filo pastry from its packaging and cover with a moist cloth or clear film (plastic wrap). Place one sheet of filo pastry on a board and brush generously with melted butter. Fold the buttered pastry sheet in half lengthways, brush with some more butter and fold lengthways again.

5 Place about 15ml/1 tbsp of the vegetable filling on the bottom right-hand corner of the pastry sheet and fold over to form a triangle. Continue to fold to the top of the sheet, maintaining the triangular shape. Moisten the ends and seal the edges. Place on the prepared baking sheet and brush with some melted butter. Make the rest of the samosas in the same way. Bake just below the top of the oven for 20 minutes or until browned.

Makes 12

60ml/4 tbsp sunflower oil or plain olive oil

1.5ml/¼ tsp asafoetida

2.5ml/½ tsp black mustard seeds

5ml/1 tsp cumin seeds

2.5ml/½ tsp nigella seeds

1 medium-sized onion, finely chopped

2 green chillies, finely chopped (seeded if you like)

2.5ml/½ tsp ground turmeric

5ml/1 tsp ground cumin

350g/12oz boiled potatoes, cut into bitesize pieces

110g/4oz/1 cup fresh peas, cooked or frozen peas, thawed

50g/2oz/½ cup carrots, coarsely grated

5ml/1 tsp salt or to taste

2.5ml/½ tsp garam masala

30ml/2 tbsp fresh coriander (cilantro) leaves, chopped

12 sheets filo pastry, each about 18cm x 29cm/7in x 11in

75g/3oz/6 tbsp butter, melted

PER PORTION Energy 180kcal/752kJ; Protein 3.6g; Carbohydrate 19.6g, of which sugars 2.5g; Fat 10.4g, of which saturates 4.1g; Cholesterol 26mg; Calcium 38mg; Fibre 1.6g; Sodium 58mg.

Medley of Vegetables with Dumplings
Oondhiu

This is a fabulous mixture of fresh vegetables such as potatoes, green beans, aubergines, sweet potatoes and bananas, cooked with spicy gram flour dumplings and enhanced by the distinctive flavour of dried fenugreek leaves. This recipe provides a healthy and substantial vegetarian main course.

1 For the dumplings: put the gram flour into a mixing bowl and add the remaining dumpling ingredients, up to and including the coriander leaves. Mix thoroughly and add the hot oil, lime juice and water. Mix until a stiff dough is formed and knead it for about a minute. Divide the dough into 10 equal balls. Heat the oil in a wok or other suitable pan for deep-frying over a medium heat. Fry the dumplings until they are crisp and golden brown. Drain on kitchen paper and set aside.

2 For the vegetable curry: grind the coconut in a coffee grinder and mix in a bowl with the coriander, 10ml/2 tsp of the garlic, 10ml/2 tsp of the ginger, the chilli powder and turmeric. Add 150ml/4fl oz/½ cup water and stir until it forms a paste. Alternatively, put the coconut in 150ml/4fl oz/½ cup water, bring to the boil and allow to cool, then purée in a blender along with the spices. Set the purée aside.

3 Heat the oil over a medium heat and add the asafoetida followed by the remaining garlic and ginger, and cook until they begin to brown. Add the coconut spice paste, increase the heat slightly, and cook for 3–4 minutes, stirring.

4 Add the potatoes to the pan and pour in 450ml/16fl oz/1¾ cups warm water. Bring the mixture to the boil, reduce the heat to low, cover the pan and cook for 7–8 minutes. Add the aubergine and sweet potato, bring back to the boil, reduce the heat to medium, cover and cook for 5–6 minutes. Add the green beans and the banana slices, cover and cook for 4–5 minutes. Add the dumplings and cook for 3–4 minutes longer. Remove from the heat and serve with any Indian bread.

Serves 4

For the dumplings:

125g/4½oz/generous 1 cup gram flour

1.5ml/¼ tsp salt

Pinch of bicarbonate of soda (baking soda)

2.5ml/½ tsp aniseed

30ml/2 tbsp dried fenugreek leaves

1 green chilli, finely chopped (seeded if you like)

15ml/1 tbsp coriander (cilantro) leaves, finely chopped

15ml/1 tbsp hot oil

15ml/1 tbsp lime juice

15ml/1 tbsp water

Oil for deep frying

For the vegetable curry:

50g/2oz desiccated (dry unsweetened shredded) coconut

10ml/2 tsp ground coriander

20ml/4 tsp garlic purée

20ml/4 tsp ginger purée

5ml/1 tsp chilli powder or to taste

5ml/1 tsp ground turmeric

30ml/2 tbsp sunflower oil or plain olive oil

1.5ml/¼ tsp asafoetida

200g/7oz potatoes, cut into 2.5cm/1in cubes

200g/7oz aubergine (eggplant), cut into 2.5cm/1in chunks

150g/5oz sweet potato, cut into 2.5cm/1in cubes

125g/4½oz green beans, cut into 2.5cm/1in lengths

2 unripe bananas, thickly sliced

PER PORTION Energy 523kcal/2182kJ; Protein 7.8g; Carbohydrate 47.6g, of which sugars 5.8g; Fat 35.1g, of which saturates 9.8g; Cholesterol 0mg; Calcium 98mg; Fibre 5.8g; Sodium 30mg.

Black-eyed Beans in Coconut and Tamarind Sauce

Feijoada

This recipe originates from the Christian community of Goa. The black-eyed beans are packed with protein and other nutrients that provide a well-balanced vegetarian diet. Ginger, garlic, chilli and onions make up the basic flavours of the sauce, which is enriched with coconut milk and the tart taste of tamarind.

1 Put the rinsed, drained black-eyed beans in a pan and pour in the coconut milk, salt and tamarind concentrate. If you are using lemon juice instead of tamarind, do not add it yet.

2 Blend the gram flour with a little water, making sure there are no lumps, and add it to the beans. Stir over a low heat and let it all simmer for 5–6 minutes.

3 Meanwhile, heat the oil in a small pan over a medium heat and add the onion. Fry, stirring regularly, until the onion begins to brown. Add the ginger and garlic, and continue to cook for a further 2–3 minutes, stirring. Add the coriander, turmeric and chilli powder. Cook for about a minute longer, then pour the spice mixture over the beans. If you are using lemon juice instead of tamarind, add it now. Stir well, remove from the heat and transfer the mixture to a serving dish. Garnish with the toasted flaked coconut and serve with plain basmati rice.

Serves 4

700g/1½lb/4½ cups canned black-eyed beans, drained and rinsed

400ml/14fl oz/1½ cups coconut milk

5ml/1 tsp salt or to taste

5ml/1 tsp tamarind concentrate or 25ml/1½ tbsp lemon juice

5ml/1 tsp gram flour

60ml/4 tbsp sunflower oil or plain olive oil

1 large onion, finely chopped

10ml/2 tsp ginger purée

10ml/2 tsp garlic purée

10ml/2 tsp ground coriander

5ml/1 tsp ground turmeric

5–7.5ml/1–1½ tsp chilli powder

To garnish:

Toasted flaked coconut

PER PORTION Energy 354kcal/1487kJ; Protein 14.3g; Carbohydrate 48.9g, of which sugars 19.6g; Fat 12.7g, of which saturates 1.7g; Cholesterol 0mg; Calcium 193mg; Fibre 13g; Sodium 797mg.

Serves 4

125g/4½oz/¾ cup skinless split chickpeas (channa dhal)

225g/8oz potatoes, peeled and cut into 2.5cm/1in cubes

125g/4½oz carrots, scraped and cut into 2.5cm/1in chunks

1 large aubergine (eggplant), cut into 2.5cm/1in chunks

30ml/2 tbsp dill leaves, roughly chopped

250g/9oz fresh spinach, roughly chopped

5ml/1 tsp salt or to taste

225g/8oz chopped canned tomatoes with their juice

60ml/4 tbsp sunflower oil or plain olive oil

1 medium onion, finely chopped

10ml/2 tsp ginger purée

10ml/2 tsp garlic purée

2 green chillies, finely chopped (seeded if you like)

2.5ml/½ tsp ground turmeric

To garnish:

1 small tomato, cut into julienne strips

PER PORTION Energy 336kcal/1406kJ; Protein 12.2g; Carbohydrate 42.7g, of which sugars 16g; Fat 14.1g, of which saturates 1.7g; Cholesterol 0mg; Calcium 214mg; Fibre 9.6g; Sodium 124mg.

Vegetables and Split Chickpeas in Spinach Sauce

Sai Bhaji

This is the national dish of Sindh, in the Indus Valley, which is the site of the world's most ancient civilization. A selection of different vegetables mixed with split chickpeas (channa dhal) are cooked together until they reach a soft, pulpy texture. A final tadka (seasoning) of onion, ginger, garlic and chillies completes the dish.

1 Wash the chickpeas and soak them for 30–60 minutes, then drain. Put them into a pan with the potatoes, carrots, aubergine and dill. Pour in 425ml/15fl oz/1¾ cups water and bring it to the boil. Reduce the heat to low, cover and simmer for 15 minutes.

2 Add the spinach and salt and stir for a minute or two until the spinach has wilted. Cover the pan and cook for 10–15 minutes, then remove from the heat. Mash the vegetables lightly, making sure that the potatoes are mashed well in order to thicken the sauce. Add the chopped tomatoes and return the pan to the heat. Cook for 2–3 minutes and set aside.

3 In a separate pan, heat the oil over a medium heat and fry the onion, ginger, garlic and green chillies, stirring regularly, until the mixture begins to brown. Stir in the turmeric and add this spice mixture to the vegetables. Stir to mix thoroughly and transfer to a serving dish. Garnish with the julienne strips of tomato and serve with boiled rice or any Indian bread.

Whole-wheat Rolls with Spicy Lentils

Dhal Baatis

From the desert region of Rajasthan, this recipe uses ghee and yogurt instead of water. These rolls are served with spiced lentils and generous amounts of ghee, which is best for the traditional flavour, but sunflower oil or plain olive oil can be used instead.

1 To make baatis: put the flour, semolina, baking powder and salt in a large mixing bowl and stir to mix. Beat the melted ghee or butter and the yogurt together and add to the flour. Mix with your fingertips and gradually add 150ml/5fl oz/⅔ cup water. Mix until a dough is formed. Transfer the dough to a flat surface and knead until it has absorbed all the moisture – it will be quite sticky at first. Cover it with a damp cloth and leave for 30 minutes.

2 Pre-heat the oven to 190°C/375°F/Gas 5.

3 Make the dough into marble-sized balls. Pour enough oil into a roasting pan to cover the base to about 5mm/¼in depth, heat it over a medium heat and add the wheat balls (baatis) in a single layer. Shake the pan so that all the balls are coated with the fat. Roast in the centre of the oven until crisp and well browned, about 20 minutes, turning them over at least twice so that they brown evenly on all sides.

4 To make dhal: wash the mung beans and the split peas and soak them separately for 4–5 hours. Drain well and place the mung beans in a pan with 1.2 litres/2 pints/5 cups water. Bring to the boil, reduce the heat to medium and partially cover the pan. Cook for 10–12 minutes, then add the drained split chickpeas. Bring back to the boil, cover and simmer for 20–25 minutes longer. Add the salt, mash some of the beans and peas with the back of a spoon and mix well. Switch off the heat.

5 Melt the ghee or butter over a low heat and fry the onion, stirring regularly, for 4–5 minutes until softened. Add the ginger and garlic and cook for 1 minute. Add the turmeric, chilli powder, coriander and cumin, stir-fry for about a minute and add this spice mixture to the cooked dhal. Re-heat the dhal and spices over a low heat, stirring well, then add the garam masala, lime juice and coriander leaves. Stir to mix well and remove from the heat.

6 To serve, place a portion of the dhal in a bowl and top with as many baatis as you wish.

Serves 4

For the baatis:

300g/10½oz/2½ cups wholemeal (whole-wheat) flour

50g/2oz/⅓ cup semolina

2.5ml/½ tsp baking powder

2.5ml/½ tsp salt

50g/2oz/4 tbsp ghee or unsalted butter, melted

75g/3oz/⅓ cup full-fat (whole) natural (plain) yogurt

Oil for roasting

For the dhal:

150g/5oz/scant 1 cup whole mung beans (sabut mung dhal)

75g/3oz/½ cup skinless split chickpeas (channa dhal)

5ml/1 tsp salt or to taste

25g/1oz/2 tbsp ghee or unsalted butter

1 medium onion, finely chopped

10ml/2 tsp ginger purée

10ml/2 tsp garlic purée

2.5ml/½ tsp ground turmeric

2.5–5ml/½–1 tsp chilli powder

5ml/1 tsp ground coriander

5ml/1 tsp ground cumin

2.5ml/½ tsp garam masala

Juice of 1 lime

30ml/2 tbsp coriander (cilantro) leaves

PER PORTION Energy 820kcal/3439kJ; Protein 27.6g; Carbohydrate 101.3g, of which sugars 10g; Fat 36.8g, of which saturates 11.1g; Cholesterol 2mg; Calcium 136mg; Fibre 11.2g; Sodium 300mg.

Serves 4

450g/1lb potatoes

60ml/4 tbsp of sunflower oil or light olive oil

2.5ml/½ tsp black mustard seeds

1 large onion, finely chopped

4–5 large garlic cloves, crushed

2.5–5ml/½–1 tsp chilli powder

5ml/1 tsp salt or to taste

25ml/1½ tbsp tamarind juice or lime juice

PER PORTION Energy 135kcal/568kJ; Protein 4g; Carbohydrate 29.3g, of which sugars 8.5g; Fat 1.1g, of which saturates 0.2g; Cholesterol 0mg; Calcium 45mg; Fibre 2.9g; Sodium 18mg.

Potatoes in Chilli-tamarind Sauce

Batata Saung

Boiled and cubed potatoes are tossed in a chilli-hot tamarind sauce that is flavoured with onion and a generous amount of crushed garlic. This dish makes a delicious accompaniment to any meal. It is essential to boil the potatoes in their skin in order to preserve the starch content. They can be boiled in advance, cooled and refrigerated. They are also much easier to cut into neater pieces once chilled.

1 Boil the potatoes in their skins, cool, peel and cut into 2.5cm/1in cubes.

2 Heat the oil over a medium heat and add the mustard seeds. As soon as they pop, add the onion and fry, stirring regularly, until the onion is golden brown. Add the garlic and cook for 2 minutes, stirring.

3 Add the cooked potatoes, chilli powder and salt. Stir to mix thoroughly. Add 150ml/5fl oz/ ½ cup warm water and cook over a medium heat for 3–4 minutes, then stir in the tamarind juice or lime juice and remove from the heat. Serve immediately.

Leeks with Garlic, Chilli and Gram Flour

Jhunko

Traditionally in this recipe, a large amount of sliced onion is sautéed with garlic and chillies, and gram flour is added at the end to soak up all the juices. The mixture is then stir-fried until the gram flour releases its nutty, toasted aroma. I have used leeks instead of onions for a slightly more subtle flavour.

1 In a non-stick wok or frying pan, heat the oil over a medium heat. When it is quite hot, but not smoking, throw in the mustard seeds, followed by the cumin seeds.

2 Add the leeks, red pepper, turmeric, chilli powder and salt. Increase the heat slightly and stir-fry the vegetables for 4–5 minutes.

3 Sprinkle the gram flour into the pan and stir-fry for a further minute. Remove from the heat and serve with any plain curry.

Serves 4

60ml/4 tbsp sunflower oil or olive oil

2.5ml/½ tsp black mustard seeds

5ml/1 tsp cumin seeds

450g/1lb young leeks, finely sliced

1 small red (bell) pepper, cut into 2.5cm/1in strips

2.5ml/½ tsp ground turmeric

2.5ml/½ tsp chilli powder

2.5ml/½ tsp salt or to taste

50g/2oz/½ cup gram flour, sifted

PER PORTION Energy 177kcal/738kJ; Protein 3.5g; Carbohydrate 14.3g, of which sugars 2.7g; Fat 12.2g, of which saturates 1.5g; Cholesterol 0mg; Calcium 51mg; Fibre 2.9g; Sodium 4mg.

Yellow Rice

Peela Bhat

Tinged with turmeric, this yellow rice is delicately spiced with a small quantity of cinnamon and cloves. The earthy taste and musky aroma of turmeric, combined with its astounding health benefits, make this rice a wonderful, nutritious change from plain boiled rice, and it is the perfect accompaniment to any vegetarian dish.

1 Wash the rice until the water runs clear, soak it for 20 minutes, then drain.

2 Heat the ghee or butter and oil over a low heat and add the cinnamon and cloves. Allow them to sizzle for 25–30 seconds, then stir in the turmeric, followed by the drained rice.

3 Stir-fry the rice for 2 minutes. Pour in 450ml/16fl oz/1¾ cups warm water and add the salt. Bring it to the boil and allow to boil steadily for 2 minutes.

4 Reduce the heat to very low, cover the pan and cook for 8 minutes. Switch off the heat and let it stand undisturbed for 20–25 minutes. Fluff up the rice with a fork and serve with the dish of your choice.

Serves 4

225g/8oz/generous 1 cup basmati rice

15ml/1 tbsp ghee or 10ml/2 tsp butter and 10ml/2 tsp plain olive oil

2.5cm/1in piece of cinnamon stick

5 cloves

2.5ml/½ tsp ground turmeric

2.5ml/½ tsp salt or to taste

PER PORTION Energy 239kcal/995kJ; Protein 4.3g; Carbohydrate 45.2g, of which sugars 0g; Fat 4.2g, of which saturates 1.8g; Cholesterol 0mg; Calcium 13mg; Fibre 0g; Sodium 1mg.

Makes 8

450g/1lb chapati flour (atta) or fine wholemeal (whole-wheat) flour

5ml/1 tsp salt or to taste

30ml/2 tbsp dried fenugreek leaves (kasuri methi)

2.5–5ml/½–1 tsp chilli powder

2.5ml/½ tsp ground turmeric

2.5ml/½ tsp ground cumin

45ml/3 tbsp sunflower oil or plain olive oil

250–300ml/9–10fl oz/generous 1 cup warm water

Oil for shallow frying

PER PORTION Energy 279kcal/1171kJ; Protein 7.4g; Carbohydrate 36.6g, of which sugars 1.2g; Fat 12.5g, of which saturates 1.4g; Cholesterol 0mg; Calcium 25mg; Fibre 5.1g; Sodium 248mg.

Wholemeal Flat Bread with Fenugreek Leaves

Methi na Thepla

This is a delicious spiced chapati from Gujarat where they serve it with meals, and also as a snack (farsan). In a Gujarati home, fresh fenugreek leaves are the obvious choice, but dried ones are more easily available elsewhere and make a lovely aromatic alternative.

1 Sift the flour into a large mixing bowl and add the salt, fenugreek leaves, chilli powder, turmeric and cumin. Mix the ingredients thoroughly with your fingertips. Now rub in the oil and gradually add the water, while continuing to mix. When a dough has formed, transfer it to a flat surface, and knead until soft and pliable. Alternatively, make the dough in a food processor. Cover with a damp cloth and let it rest for 30 minutes.

2 Divide the dough into 2 equal parts and break off or cut 4 equal portions from each. Form them into smooth balls and flatten each one to a neat cake. Dust each cake lightly in flour and roll it out to a 15cm/6in circle.

3 Preheat a cast-iron griddle over a medium heat and place a flat bread on it. Cook for 30–35 seconds and turn it over. Spread about 10ml/2 tsp oil over the surface of the cooked side and turn it over again. Let it cook for about a minute or until brown patches have appeared. Spread the second side with the same amount of oil, turn it over and cook as before until brown patches appear. Transfer the bread to a plate lined with kitchen paper. Cook all the bread in the same way. You can keep it warm by wrapping it in foil lined with kitchen paper. Serve the bread on its own or with any vegetable curry.

Serves 4–5

3 x 425g/15oz cartons of full-fat
  (whole) natural (plain) yogurt

Pinch of saffron threads, pounded

15ml/1 tbsp hot milk

75g/3oz/⅔ cup caster (superfine) sugar

2.5ml/½ tsp ground cardamom

To serve:

Fresh fruits such as mango, strawberries
  or pomegranate seeds

PER PORTION Energy 260kcal/1101kJ; Protein 14.6g;
Carbohydrate 35.5g, of which sugars 35.5g; Fat 7.6g, of
which saturates 4.3g; Cholesterol 28mg; Calcium 518mg;
Fibre 0g; Sodium 205mg.

Saffron-scented Strained Yogurt Dessert

Shrikand

Shrikand is Maharashtra's famous signature dish. You will need a large quantity of yogurt, as it has to be strained to remove nearly all the liquid. Traditionally, shrikand is served with puri, a deep-fried puffed bread, but it is also good with fresh seasonal fruits.

1 Pour the yogurt on to a large, clean muslin cloth (cheesecloth). Bring together the four corners of the cloth and tie up into a knot. Hang the muslin over the sink or in a sieve (strainer) over a bowl until all the liquid has been removed. This takes up to 6 hours, so you can safely leave it overnight.

2 When the yogurt is nearly ready, soak the pounded saffron in the hot milk for 10 minutes.

3 Untie the muslin cloth and empty the strained yogurt solids into a mixing bowl, then beat it until smooth. Add the sugar, cardamom and saffron milk along with all the threads of saffron. Mix well and chill for at least 2 hours. Serve in stemmed glasses, either in alternate layers of yogurt and fruit, or topped with the fruit of your choice.

Milky Orange Dessert

Santara ni Basundi

Basundi is a sweet, milky dessert that works well with most fruits. As the traditional cooking method is rather time-consuming, I have opted for a quicker version that uses evaporated and condensed milk, as well as ground rice, to speed up the thickening process.

1 Lightly grease the base of a heavy pan and pour both types of milk into it. Mix well and place over a medium heat.

2 Blend the ground rice with just enough water to make a pouring consistency, and add it to the milk when it comes to boiling point. Cook gently, stirring constantly, for 10–12 minutes until the mixture has thickened to a creamy consistency. Remove from the heat, cool and chill for 4–5 hours.

3 Stir in the orange juice, ground cardamom and nutmeg, then stir in half the mandarin segments. Transfer the basundi to stemmed glasses and garnish with the remaining mandarin segments and the mint sprigs.

Serves 4

400g/14oz canned evaporated milk

400g/14oz canned sweetened condensed milk

15ml/1 tbsp ground rice

Juice of 2–3 large oranges

5ml/1 tsp ground cardamom

1.5ml/¼ tsp freshly grated nutmeg

300g/10½oz canned mandarin segments, drained

To decorate:

3–4 fresh mint sprigs

PER PORTION Energy 482kcal/2032kJ; Protein 17.1g; Carbohydrate 75.8g, of which sugars 73.8g; Fat 14.2g, of which saturates 8.8g; Cholesterol 53mg; Calcium 566mg; Fibre 0.3g; Sodium 262mg.

Index